Let Go of What Hurts You

How to Heal from the Past and Free Yourself Through Awareness, Self-Love, and a Positive Mindset

Lara Spadetto

Contents

To my mother Cristina who has always given me unconditional Love, and to my children Stefano, Filippo, and Ilaria who are my North Star and show me the path to follow every day.

"The past is a source of knowledge, and the
future is a source of hope."
—Stephen Ambrose

Introduction

W hen I was younger and still in school, I remember carrying a backpack full of heavy textbooks on my way home one afternoon. I knew it was heavy, but I didn't realize just how heavy it was until, finally making it home, I took off my backpack and set it down on the floor.

At that moment, I understood what people meant when they described things as being a "real weight off their shoulders." I felt lighter than air, like my posture had straightened, and I was suddenly two inches taller. It was easy to walk, suddenly; easy to stand up tall and step lightly, unburdened by the heavy load I had been carrying.

It wasn't until I was older—much older—that I felt that sensation again, though this time it wasn't due to any physical cause. Much as I hadn't realized how heavy my backpack was when I was a child, I hadn't realized how heavy the mental pain and trauma I had accrued in my adulthood was. I hadn't realized just how much of a burden I had been shouldering until, one day, I felt lighter.

That's what trauma can do to you. More to the point, that's what life can do to you. It has a way of turning you upside down. I have, at times, felt as though life was dragging me down into a dark vortex; a whirlpool from which I could not escape.

As life confronts us with difficult trials, our past traumas, beliefs, and the fear of change work in tandem to hold us back, keeping us in a state of immobility. At times, it can feel like we want to keep the pain. The storm we experience prevents us from letting go and, in time, can generate a seemingly endless cycle; a vicious, ever-turning circle that prevents us from finding our way out from the dark.

I've known many people who have shared this same feeling at some point in their lives. I asked myself: If so many of us are experiencing the same thing, why is it so hard to escape this storm? When I was in the darkness, even as I reached for help, even as other hands reached for me, nothing seemed to be able to pull me free.

It wasn't until I was out of life's turbulence with my shoulders squared, standing tall and feeling lighter than I had in years, that I realized the answer to my question. This is because, as impossible as it might seem when you're inside the dark spiral, the first steps toward freedom are looking within yourself. It is through this inward gaze that we can take our lives into our own hands, wrestling back control from the vortex and giving it back to ourselves.

Once we find the help within ourselves by tapping into our inner strength and power, we begin our journey towards healing. The only way out of the darkness is to allow ourselves to be guided by our inner light. By removing our mental burden, we can move forward, piece by piece.

As was the case with me, and as may very well be the case with you, we often don't realize just how weighted down we've been. That's the remarkable thing about humans—we adapt. We learn to live with things; even the bad things. But the truth is that, eventually, you don't have to live with these things any longer. We can slowly but surely begin to let them go in time.

I have endured trauma and hardships throughout my life that left wounds which took a long time to heal. But here is the crucial thing I hope you remember: They healed. Through these experiences, I learned valuable lessons about the power of optimism, perseverance, and the continuous and sometimes life-long journey toward getting better. I have spent so much time and effort working towards creating a bright future for myself that I now feel confident and capable when facing life's challenges.

I know, as well, that you are capable of this, too. After all, you have lived through your worst days and come out the other side. The you that you were when experiencing trauma and hardships was strong enough to get you through that time of suffering. You have always had the strength to overcome adversity, even when you did not realize that strength.

Finding this strength to move forward and leave the past where it belongs—which is in the past—can be challenging. There are times when it might feel next to impossible. But I promise you, it's possible; it only takes a bit of effort and willpower. Throughout my journey, I have learned many techniques, behaviors, ways of thinking, and mindsets that I have used to help me release the burden of pain and finally feel free.

It can be hard when we're in the vortex. We put up defenses, both consciously and unconsciously. We use these defenses to protect ourselves from real and perceived enemies. While these defenses might genuinely protect us during difficult times, they can also hurt us when those hard times are over. Have you ever responded defensively to an innocuous comment, lashing out when it might not be deserved? I know I have. This is because of these defenses we have built.

Our minds are incessantly working, leading us to a state of hypervigilance and constant alert. We linger on pain, on what and who has hurt us, and as a result, we become overwhelmed with feelings of anger, betrayal, and thoughts of revenge. While sometimes these thoughts and feelings can be a driving force, that's not a sustainable way to live. Eventually, you'll burn yourself out, falling back into old pain patterns.

It's only through recognizing these thoughts, feelings, and behaviors that we can move forward. Recognizing them, objectifying them, and taking the time to reflect on them are the first steps on your journey. When you do this, you are faced with a decision: To hold on to your pain, or to try and let go. It's only when you choose to let go that you can begin the—perhaps not simple, but certainly necessary—path towards true inner freedom.

Throughout this book, I will share with you everything that I have learned on my journey of healing from the past; from growing in awareness, understanding our present situations and past pain, and coping techniques and strategies to transform self-pity into self-love. All of these lessons are ones that I know will guide you with care, as you begin to let go of what hurts you and heal from your past.

Chapter 1

Acceptance

What is right in my situation that I'm not getting

"Happiness can exist only in acceptance."
—*George Orwell*

As often happens, the trials that life gives us are unexpected. So it was for me in 2021. What was certain to me was suddenly gone, and my world seemed upside down.

When you flounder as you're carried by the current, you try to find holds to cling to that can give you help and answers. Among the many friends who helped me during that time, one in particular gave me a piece of advice that, for me, was a turning point.

I met my friend a few years earlier while I was living in Abu Dhabi, she was my Reiki teacher at the time.

I wrote her a short message telling her about the turbulent moment I was experiencing and asking for advice. She told me to repeat the following words even though the meaning might not be clear: "What's right in my situation that I'm not getting?"

She told me not to look for an answer, but instead to ask the question as many times as possible for a few days. She assured me that I would soon have clarity. It wasn't the answer I was expecting; a question to answer the flurry of questions I had in my head?

But hey, what did I have to lose?

I decided to follow her advice and repeat that mantra in my head several times, to see it as some kind of magic formula.

Obviously, the clarity did not arrive immediately. Little by little some pieces fit together perfectly; others though, even now, are struggling to find a place. I know that sooner or later they will find their space, when the time is right for me. I know that the path I am taking can lead me to growth if I take the reins of my thoughts, or to stagnation if I do not let it flow. And I know that what happens is not always what we want, but perhaps it is what we need to evolve to the point of view of a whole vision.

Accepting what life gives us, even when what it offers seems like unmotivated pain, is the first step. No, it's not simple. Indeed, it's very complex, because it is above all an interior work. But there is no point in living in denial or ignoring difficulties; the essential thing is to face these challenges as they arise and learn to consciously let go of what causes us unnecessary pain. This is the only way to free ourselves from the invisible chains that prevent our growth.

After all, life has a certain number of days, but we are not allowed to know how many. Is it useful to waste some of them thinking and rethinking what hurts us?

Is it healthy to self-inflict suffering that is caused only by our thoughts?

This does not mean you can or should avoid suffering. Unpleasant emotions such as grief, pain, and anger should be experienced. They are a part of you and are normal responses to your life circumstances. Instead of trying to ignore these negative feelings, acknowledge them. Take some time to recognize what your mind is experiencing and then, as a distant observer, learn to accept. When we look at our emotions objectively, it becomes easier to understand how to deal with them. It is only by taking a step back that we can begin to see the way forward. When you ask yourself, "What's right in my situation that I'm not getting," you're taking that step back.

Our emotions can affect our way of thinking and, therefore, our way of being and living. But it is also true that our thoughts can keep us in a particular emotional state. Understanding which thoughts to cultivate and let blossom, and which ones to cut can help us on our inner journey. Cutting ties can be as cathartic as mending bridges, especially when it comes to freeing ourselves from the negative thoughts that can so often flood and overwhelm our minds.

The Challenges of Life

What is truly fascinating about life is that you can never be in total control of it. You can have plans for a project in the future, try to imagine what it will be like, but then, life happens.

So, what can we do? As long as the unexpected is something positive, we accept it without reservation. But when something tragic or painful occurs, we get down, perceive this lack of direction, and feel that our internal compass has lost its North Star.

And this is where we really come into play; where the leading role is given to our ability to respond to adversity. And it's also where we are given the challenge.

You have probably already heard the saying, "everything happens for a reason," a phrase perhaps too often abused, because it is undoubtedly tough to accept this motivation when we are living in dark times and are in the midst of the storm. How could there be a reason for losing someone you love, for divorce, family conflicts, extreme lifestyle changes, or other trials?

Even when we try to avoid these challenges, we can find ourselves miserable, sometimes even making the situations worse. It can feel like there's no winning; like no matter what you do, you're doomed to fail. It's understandable to wonder how any of this could have any purpose, reason, or value at all when going through times like these.

But it's thoughts like that which keep you in the storm. When you resent what you have been through, you create roadblocks in your mind, cutting off any chance to get out of the terrible place you have found yourself in. Focusing on what has and still does hurt you means you cannot focus on what brings you peace.

When dealing with the residual pain born of life's challenges, try to reframe your way of thinking. Instead of resenting these moments, face them head-on and accept them. They are in the past, and since there's no such thing as time travel, no one can change the past. What happened happened, and while you can't change that, you can hold on to the fact that it is not still happening.

Try, if you can, to think of a moment that recently brought you a sense of joy, happiness, or peace. Maybe you watched the sunrise. Maybe you treated yourself to a meal you love, but don't normally eat. Maybe you saw a friend, read a book, or watched a movie you enjoyed. Remember that you lived through all of that hardship, all of that pain, and made it to these moments.

It's also essential to remember that you did not only accrue pain through the challenges and adversity that you have lived through, you also grew and changed as a person. There's a reason we refer to it as overcoming adversity. Your past is not something you lived through, it is something you were able to overcome; something you were able to rise against and survive, perhaps weary, perhaps a bit battered, but you survived all the same. You found that you were stronger than you may have ever known by undergoing these challenges. You are, and always have been, strong enough to make it through the storm.

By accepting what happened in our lives, we can begin to take the first steps to free ourselves from our pain. Let it live in the past as a distant memory and start to let go. You can't change the past. You can't know the future. You can't control life. But what you do have power over is the present moment; your choices, actions, commitments, and resolve are tools you can use in your journey towards healing.

There are so many possibilities in front of you. Even at this moment, your life is filled with potential. You don't have to keep suffering. Just as you were strong enough to make it through life's trials, you are strong enough to let go of the pain those trials brought you. There are endless possibilities before you. All you have to do is choose which path is yours to take.

Dealing With Resentment and Anger

It's easy to say that the way to move forward is to learn to acknowledge, accept, and then release negative and troubling emotions like anger, bitterness, jealousy, and resentment. In practice, though, that's a difficult task; one many people find themselves struggling to achieve.

However, just because something is difficult doesn't make it impossible. Over the years, I have learned several powerful and helpful coping mechanisms and techniques that assisted me in learning to manage the resentment and anger in my life.

Speak Your Feelings Aloud

Whether it's talking to another person, talking to your reflection, or just expressing your thoughts and feelings, conveying your emotions aloud is an excellent way to deal with anger and resentment.

Have you ever spoken to yourself out loud? I know I have, especially when trying to remember something. When we talk aloud, it validates what we are doing, thinking, and feeling. Audibly stating your inner thoughts and emotions can take what lives in your mind and give it form outside of your mind. In a way, it makes what you are experiencing feel real.

By verbalizing your feelings, you validate your emotions. This validation of what you are feeling can significantly help you in the process of accepting what you're feeling. We try to pretend they aren't there, especially with the so-called 'ugly' emotions. This, however, only feeds the anger and resentment in your heart. We acknowledge that these emotions exist by being honest with ourselves and putting our feelings into words.

Speaking aloud can also help you work through tangles in your thought patterns. It can help you pinpoint why you are feeling angry or resentful and help you realize the times when your anger may not be the best response. By giving a voice to your anger, you can untangle it from the other emotions that often hide beneath the anger; emotions like fear, pain, or hurt. This, in turn, will help you learn to respond to these other emotions in a way that does not involve anger or resentment.

Reframe Your Thinking

Many of our difficulties with letting go of pain and trauma can stem from how we have learned to respond to that trauma. Our learned patterns of thinking and behavior so often keep us trapped in the cycles of pain.

When we learn to change our thought patterns, we free ourselves from these negative behaviors and coping mechanisms. This concept, the one involving us learning how to reshape our thinking, is the core of cognitive-behavioral therapy, or CBT. This therapy focuses on the present life rather than past traumas, emphasizing the importance of learning how to manage your current self so you can move forward healthily.

The practice of reframing your thinking isn't only limited to CBT, either. This practice can be seen in mindfulness routines, as well as in practices of gratitude. However, through all these different practices, the core of the importance of changing the way we allow our thoughts to flow remains the same.

The first step in reframing your thinking is recognizing when you fall into downward spirals. As resentment and anger so often come from bitterness towards past painful experiences, it's easy to fall into the habit of constantly picking at the memories of that time. When you find yourself doing this, stop in your tracks. Remind yourself to focus on something else, even something trivial. Try playing a game on your phone, going for a walk, or calling a friend.

This can be difficult at first, but, as with everything, time will make it easier. Eventually, you will be more able to recognize and break free from negative thought patterns. Once you do this, you can reroute those thoughts towards a healthier and more positive mindset.

Practice Mindfulness

Mindfulness is a practice centered around the idea of being intensely rooted in the present moment. It emphasizes living entirely in the present and not allowing yourself to become distracted by thoughts and worries regarding the past or the future.

The act of practicing mindfulness spans many techniques and exercises. One of the most famous mindfulness techniques is meditation. This includes many forms of meditation, from traditional sitting and breathing meditations to moving meditations, like yoga or tai chi.

Mindfulness is about more than meditation, though! When we practice mindfulness, we are encouraged to connect with and understand our thoughts and feelings. When you find yourself experiencing anger or resentment, try to breathe deeply. Focus on what you are feeling, and take some time to feel the emotion truly.

Once you have done this, examine the emotion. The deep breaths will help calm your mind, freeing you from the impulsivity that often goes hand in hand with feelings like anger. This calm control will help you to separate your resentment from the present moment, allowing you to let it drift back to the past.

Journaling

Journaling is another excellent way to help you manage your anger and resentment. Writing down your thoughts is a great way to help you identify thought patterns, triggers, and any self-sabotaging you might be engaging in without even realizing.

Similar to speaking your thoughts aloud, writing your thoughts down—particularly those related to feelings of anger and resentment—can help you validate these emotions while also understanding their root. So often, even when anger is justified, we lose our rationality. By engaging in the practice of journaling, you can begin to employ logic to combat the gut reactions born from the anger or resentment you have experienced.

You can also use journaling as a form of catharsis. If there is someone you have resentment towards in your life but cannot confront or speak with for whatever reason, try writing them a letter. In doing this, you will be able to put down all of the complicated feelings you have towards that person in words, expelling them from your body and leaving them on the page.

Once you have written this letter, you can do whatever you like with it. Some people might hold on to it, while others might tear it up or even burn it as a symbolic act of freeing themselves from those resentments. Either way, by putting pen to paper, you can more easily work through your feelings regarding someone. By sealing those feelings into a letter, you can finally feel as though you have had your say and begin to let go.

Channel Your Emotions Through Healthy Hobbies

Channeling your emotions through healthy and positive habits and hobbies is another excellent way to deal with anger and resentment in your life. Exercise is a typical example of one of these hobbies, but having said that, I must honestly point out that being particularly lazy myself, my favorite exercise is simply walking in the countryside. It doesn't require too much effort, and it frees my mind. Other healthy hobbies include painting, crafting, baking, creative writing, or playing an instrument. You could even engage in volunteering or getting involved in various causes that are important to you.

Whatever the case, you can better learn to cope with these feelings by using a healthy outlet to channel and express your emotions. Instead of allowing yourself to wallow in your negative feelings, engaging in a healthy hobby will help you break free from self-pity, bitterness, and stress. More than that, having a hobby can bring pleasure and joy into your life, helping you to achieve a new, positive perspective.

<hr />

Your Perception Is Critical

Having the right perspective can often make all the difference in life. You've probably heard of the "power of positive thinking" before. The theory behind this phrase is not to minimize the suffering and hardships people have undergone, but rather to emphasize that we have power over our thoughts and can use that power to promote a mindset and outlook of positivity, rather than negativity. We actively reject resentment, bitterness, and the pain of old hardships by choosing positivity. Indeed, through positive thinking, we open ourselves up to experiencing the world with an open and optimistic mindset.

Think back to a time when you were faced with a new experience; maybe you were moving to a new town, or you were starting a new job. Did you go into this new experience thinking everything would go wrong, or did you go into it with high hopes for a fresh start? More often than not, going into new experiences with a negative mindset will make us more likely to see negativity in the experience. On the other hand, going into new experiences with a positive mind will lead us to have positive experiences.

There was a study which followed 70,000 women from 2004 t0 2012 and found that, of these women, those with an optimistic attitude not only had a better life socially, but physically as well, with many of these women having a significantly lower risk of heart disease, stroke, and cancer (Kim et al., 2016).

It's incredible, isn't it? Engaging with the world with a different perspective can so drastically change your life. When you adopt an attitude of positivity, letting go of negativity becomes exponentially easier.

There are a few strategies I have learned over the years, strategies I will share with you, that have helped me become a little more positive, hopeful, and optimistic in my everyday life. While none of these strategies are a miracle cure, they are a way to remind yourself of all the beautiful things that exist in your present situation.

Avoid Passivity

Passivity is the antithesis of mindfulness. In mindfulness, you actively engage with the present. When you are passive, you detach yourself from the moment and allow yourself to drift, mindless and aimless, through life. This detached passivity leaves your mind wide open for wallowing and ruminating on pain, hardships, and self-pity.

Try to be engaged in everything you do. This does not mean being hyper-aware, though! Rather, try to find enjoyment in all that you do. By engaging in activities that bring you pleasure or joy, you can easily stay rooted in the experience of that moment. Try to find ways to make even mindless activities engaging, too!

Take folding laundry as an example, as it's something that can be so repetitive. Listening to music, calling a loved one on the phone, or watching a movie while doing this typically mindless chore is an excellent way to avoid passivity and enjoy living in that moment.

Focus on the Good

Even when things go wrong in life, there's usually a way to find a bright side. I know there have been so many situations where something I thought was negative was actually positive. After all, there's a reason for classic sayings like, "blessing in disguise," and "every cloud has a silver lining." When we allow ourselves to be open to the good in a situation, we can more easily see the upside of unpleasant or disheartening situations.

A great way to learn to do this is to practice gratitude. Practicing gratitude is the act of noticing, acknowledging, and remembering the things in life for which we are grateful. It could be something significant, like a dear friend, or it could be something minor, like taking time in the morning to enjoy a cup of coffee.

Whatever it is, being grateful for the good things in your life helps you begin to notice other blessings in your life; blessings of which you might not have even been aware.

Celebrate Your Successes

It's easy for so many of us to want to brush off or downplay our successes. So often, we're trained to believe that being proud of ourselves is the same as being conceited or arrogant, but that couldn't be further from the truth! That way of thinking is just another way to keep you down.

Instead, celebrate yourself. Even small successes are worth celebrating. When we celebrate our accomplishments, we can acknowledge our progress in life. Making our way out of the storm of life and trauma is a challenging task, but it's done by taking another step forward. Each of these steps is something you should be proud to have accomplished.

Learn to Enjoy Time Alone

Spending time alone is a powerful thing, and it's something that, so often, people shy away from. For those of us, like you and I, who have experienced the hardships of life, taking time to yourself and, more importantly, enjoying time spent alone is a powerful thing.

It's when you spend time alone that you can begin to get to know your true self. It's easy to see yourself in a certain way, especially when you have experienced trauma, but that self-image isn't always who you are. Taking the time to get to know yourself will help you learn what an incredible, resilient, and strong person you truly are.

Surround Yourself With Positivity

Having a positive outlook comes from feeling good on the inside, but we can corroborate this by taking a little help from how we live on the outside.

One of the best ways to achieve this outlook is to surround yourself with positivity. This includes engaging in activities you enjoy, wearing clothes you like, and spending time with people who make you feel valued.

In particular, being with positive people will help you bring balance into your life. Many emotions and mentalities are almost contagious. The energy that is transmitted by other people, even if it is not tangible, is physically felt. It doesn't matter if other people's negative attitudes are voluntary or not, they devour your energy and alter your well-being.

Conversely, being with people who will uplift you instead of knocking you down—people who essentially just make you feel good—will increase your confidence and self-esteem, and help guide you to a life filled with light.

When you go through each day, do your best to practice positivity. When you find yourself struggling with managing your resentment, confronting the challenges of life, or when you need clarity and a fresh perspective, ask yourself the same question my friend asked me: What is right about my situation that I am not getting?

Chapter 2

Awareness

The power of your thoughts

"Awareness is all about restoring your freedom
to choose what you want instead of what your
past imposes on you."
—*Deepak Chopra*

"Look outside and you will see yourself. Look
inside and you will find yourself."
—*Drew Gerald*

I t's so easy to remember bad experiences. The bad
memories seem to last longer; to linger with more
clarity in your mind than the good ones ever do. This is
because our brains don't function solely to make us happy.

In fact, the primary function of our brains is to ensure our
survival. So, when we look at this from an evolutionary
and survival-based perspective, it makes sense that we
remember negative moments with greater ease. After all,

if we remember the pain, we're more likely to avoid the activities that brought us to that pain in the future.

The problem is that, while this made sense for our distant ancestors who had to survive in significantly more challenging conditions and physical situations than us, our modern lives typically don't need such an emphasis on enduring physical hardships. As such, we remember the emotional pain of these negative experiences with a precision that brings us more harm than good.

However, this doesn't have to mean your memories and bad experiences trap you. Instead, you can learn to harness and channel your negative memories, thoughts, and experiences with practice and effort. Learning to redirect these thoughts can often lead you to a greater understanding of what brings you joy, comfort, and happiness. Having an awareness of your thoughts gives you control over them, and once you have control, you can use your thoughts—both positive and negative—to your benefit.

Thought Awareness

When we feel a storm of emotions swelling within us, it's easy to become swept away; to allow the winds and torrents of the feelings to drag you back into the past. This, thankfully, doesn't have to happen. By remaining focused on the present, we can stand firm against the storm.

Thought awareness is the first step towards making it through the proverbial storm. To begin practicing it, you must first understand what it means to be self-aware.

Self-awareness theory is the idea that we are separate from our thoughts. So often, we conflate our thoughts with our identity. This theory, however, states that this isn't the case. Instead of being our thoughts, we are their observers.

In this sense, being self-aware means having the ability to separate what we think from what we are, and then, in time, understand how to sit back and observe our thoughts with a more detached perspective; one that's granted by distance.

The problem many of us struggle with—and it's something I've certainly struggled with myself—is that it can be challenging to achieve this level of awareness regarding our thoughts, particularly our negative thoughts. So often, negative thoughts flit through our minds without us even noticing. When we don't see these negative thoughts, we aren't able to challenge them, and instead, they can do unchecked harm to our state of mind.

Thought awareness is the process by which we counter the harmful effects of these negative thoughts. As we observe our thoughts, thought awareness helps us gain perspective towards what's going on in our minds and how this might be affecting our daily lives. Here are a few ways that I've found will help you develop thought awareness in your life, so that you, too, can begin to see the way your mind is working:

Focus on Something Else

Learning to focus on something else consciously can significantly help you in your journey towards developing thought awareness. When we intentionally focus on something, it takes our mind off the redundant thoughts that bring us pain and seek to hurt us. Even something as simple as watching a movie, reading a book, painting your nails, doing your hair, or cooking can help you shift your thoughts away from your pain.

After all, while we can feel many emotions simultaneously, we can't do the same with our thoughts. Have you ever tried to listen to a podcast and read a book at the same time? One of these activities will always pull your focus over the other. This is how consciously focusing your thoughts leads your mind away from negative thoughts. By choosing a different, more positive thought to be the focal point in your mind, you are banishing the painful thoughts to the back and out of the way.

Set Goals

Thinking about goals is an excellent way to divert your thinking. This is because goal-setting is not only motivational, but also action-oriented. One of the most significant issues many people who struggle with negative thoughts face is the tendency to become trapped in their heads. Having a goal to work towards gets us out of our heads, keeping us focused on the world around us, rather than the one within us.

Having goals also keeps us busy. I don't know about you, but I tend to spiral when I have too much time on my hands. While taking breaks and relaxing is undeniably essential to a healthy and happy life, having too much time off can also stand in the way of such a life.

The key to setting goals is to make them achievable and realistic. So often, we are too broad with our goals. Being specific helps us better understand what we need to do to achieve our goals. For example, instead of setting a goal like exercising more, try something like going for a walk three times a week.

Freewriting

While journaling can be an excellent tool for developing thought awareness, I want to hone in on a different writing practice that can help us understand our thoughts. Specifically, I want to show you the practice of freewriting and its ability to help you understand your thought processes, and recognize the patterns of your mind.

For those of you who might not know, freewriting is typically associated with a way for writers to practice and develop their writing. It's similar to free association games or brainstorming practices. In freewriting, you write down everything that comes to your mind, in sentences and paragraphs, without stopping or trying to organize your thoughts. You shouldn't worry about things like proper grammar or spelling, but instead, let your mind flow freely through your pen and onto the paper.

The next time you feel stressed, angry, or overwhelmed with emotion, try freewriting. As you write down all of your thoughts as they come without stopping to think about them, you'll begin to see the shape your thought processes take. The more you do this, the more you'll be able to recognize patterns, repeated thoughts, and feelings laid out on the pages before you.

By recognizing your thought patterns, you'll be better able to recognize them while they're happening. This means that whenever you have a negative thought, you'll be able to catch it and put a stop to it, before it can bring up any pain.

Reflection

Taking time to reflect on your behaviors, reactions, and experiences is another way to hone your thought awareness. Checking in with yourself, turning your gaze inwards, and analyzing situations where you experienced negative emotions will help you understand your thoughts during that time.

You can reflect in many different ways. Some people like to journal, some like to meditate, while others prefer to sit and think. Whatever the method, self-reflection is a great way to boost your self-awareness and untangle the inner workings of your mind.

It's important to remember, however, not to overdo your reflection! It's easy for those who have experienced trauma and pain to tend to overthink things. While, on the surface, overthinking and reflection might appear similar, when you look a little closer, you can see that they couldn't be further apart. Reflection involves looking at yourself with an objective and non-judgmental gaze. On the other hand, overthinking is more like wallowing and often keeps us trapped in a mire of self-loathing.

Seek an Outside Perspective

Sometimes, the best way to gain perspective is to borrow someone else's! Speaking to a friend, family member, or another outside observer can lead to moments of clarity and epiphany that we wouldn't be able to achieve on our own. Think of it as a sounding board; having someone to bounce ideas off of helps us organize our thoughts and see things in a new light. Hearing how someone else thinks can help us see how we are—or aren't—thinking in similar patterns.

Remember, though, that you don't have to agree with everything someone else has to say. While their insights can be valuable, it's essential to learn to trust your instincts as well. Depending too much on external perspective could lead to an inability to trust your view.

———————◆◯◆———————

Positive Affirmations

Once you begin to understand thought awareness, it's essential to start putting in the work to change how your negative thoughts move through your mind actively. Using positive affirmations is one such way to reprogram our minds. Affirmations are low-effort, free of cost, and effective, making them the perfect way to use your newfound thought awareness for your gain.

You've probably even used positive affirmations before without realizing it. Think of a time when you encouraged yourself, telling yourself something like, "I've got this." This is an example of a positive affirmation. If you had continued to tell yourself this, repeating it each day like a mantra, you would have noticed its long-term beneficial effects.

Positive affirmations work by reprogramming the way your mind behaves. They shift your focus from the negative to the positive, highlighting your strengths rather than your perceived weaknesses.

Our brains are capable of continual change. This is true, no matter how old you are! This is known as neuroplasticity, and it's the reason behind our brain's ability to adapt to our circumstances and situations. You're never too set in your ways to change, and neuroplasticity is proof of that.

We can encourage our brains to accept these positive, life-affirming statements as fact, simply by repeating affirmations. Even if you don't initially believe in the truth of an affirmation, the more you repeat it, the more you will begin to believe. In this way, we're not only reshaping our thoughts, but reshaping our reality.

Affirmations help us grow our self-confidence, make us feel more relaxed, and boost self-awareness. As you repeat affirmations and foster your belief in their truth, you should try to act on them. If you have been telling yourself that "you can remain calm in the face of overwhelming emotion," as the saying goes, you should try to incorporate breathing exercises into your life. These calming exercises, when paired with your affirmation, will help you achieve your affirmations' fullest potential.

You can either look up pre-written affirmations or write some of your own. Typically, writing your own makes them personalized, but if you aren't sure where to begin, there are all kinds of affirmations you can use to get started.

Either way, there are some things to keep in mind when using positive affirmations. Here are a few tips I've discovered while making the most of positive affirmations in my life:

Present Tense

You want your affirmation to remind you of the strengths that already exist within you. By speaking in the present tense, our affirmations remind our brains that we are currently capable and can help us boost our confidence.

After all, it's easier to believe in ourselves when we are continually saying how wonderful we already are.

Use "I Am" Statements

Using "I am" statements help bring legitimacy to your affirmations. It's a statement of fact; a powerful way to remind your brain that what you are saying is true. These "I am" statements give your brain a sort of order, which can help boost the effectiveness of your affirmations.

Avoid Negative Language

When using affirmations, ensure you're using positive language. Positive language motivates the brain, while negative language demoralizes our thinking.

For example, you might be struggling with fear. Saying an affirmation like "I am not afraid" isn't an effective way to overcome your fear. This is because the emphasis is placed on how you experience fear, not your ability to rise above fear. Instead, try something like "I am brave," which emphasizes what you are, rather than what you are not.

Keep It Simple

Finally, keep your affirmations simple! Short, straightforward, and easy-to-remember statements will help your brain retain the affirmation and adapt its pathways to its intention more easily. Too much information might confuse or overwhelm your mind, so keeping it simple and to the point will help your affirmation feel natural.

Meditation

Meditation is one of the best ways to promote awareness, manage stress, and gain emotional control. When we meditate, we can achieve a state of profound peace, with still minds and complete control over our thoughts. We can genuinely learn to redirect our thinking away from our pain and trauma within this meditative state, and towards a happier, healthier self.

Meditation is an old practice with all kinds of benefits and can be practiced in multiple ways. There is evidence that meditation can reduce stress, improve memory, improve sleep, and greatly benefit emotional well-being.

One study conducted on the effects of mindfulness meditation found that it can decrease a person's negative thoughts (Kiken & Shook, 2014). This underlines our ability to control our thought patterns and decrease negative thinking, as well as the effectiveness of meditation in helping us refocus our minds.

Many people think you have to follow specific rules to meditate correctly. But good news! This is actually a common misconception. You can achieve a meditative state in a myriad of different ways. You can meditate while practicing yoga, walking, or even engaging in creative activities, like painting or cooking. Below are a few of the different types of meditation:

Mantra Meditation

Mantra meditation is a practice that pairs well with positive affirmations. In this type of meditation, you direct your focus to a single word or phrase. If you have been struggling to accept a particular affirmation, this type of meditation could be of great help.

This type of meditation is excellent for when you're feeling overwhelmed, as it can help you consciously redirect your thoughts away from your emotional pain and past traumas, and towards something beneficial instead.

When engaging in mantra meditation, begin by taking a few deep breaths and allowing yourself to relax. You can do this meditation either sitting or standing, but I recommend being comfortable, regardless. As you relax, repeat your mantra in your head, over and over.

Do this for a few minutes, and allow your mind to truly focus on this mantra. If you get distracted, don't worry! It's common for minds to drift during meditation, especially if you're a beginner, but even people who have been meditating for years can experience distraction. Just redirect your thoughts back to your mantra.

Guided Meditation

Guided meditation is when someone else leads you through the meditative process. This can be through an instructor or mentor and can be done in person, virtually, or via a phone app. This might be a suitable type of meditation for you if you're a beginner, as having someone guide you through the process can make it less daunting.

A good thing about guided meditations is that they can be pretty specific. There are all kinds of guided meditations for problems like acceptance, managing stress, and improving sleep. If you find yourself struggling with a particular issue, you might find there's a guided meditation that can help you.

Moving Meditation

Moving meditation is when you are active while meditating. Yoga is a famous example of moving meditation, as you shift from stretch to stretch, all while breathing deeply and being aware of your body. Tai chi is another example of moving meditation. The key to these meditations lies in your awareness. In this sense, moving meditation is similar to mindfulness meditation, as it promotes the idea of being aware of your actions in the moment.

Moving meditation doesn't have to be a particular exercise, either! You can achieve meditative states when walking or running, especially through nature. Simply focus on what you are doing, breathe deeply, and allow your mind to be free of troubling thoughts—and you will have achieved a moving meditation.

Mindfulness Meditation

Mindfulness meditation is one of the best ways to boost awareness and control your thoughts. This form of meditation encourages us to allow our thoughts to flow without judgment. Rather than being attached to these thoughts, mindfulness meditation encourages us to let them drift through our minds, and then drift away.

This type of meditation emphasizes letting go of pain from the past, as well as fears for the future. It encourages us to focus on the present moment, fully aware of our current surroundings and immediate experiences. This type of meditation is, in many ways, the key to overcoming the storm of overwhelming emotions and pain. It is the final step in achieving thought awareness and refocusing our minds.

You can practice mindfulness meditation anywhere and at any time. If you find yourself falling into negative thinking patterns, focus on your breathing—the way the air moves into your lungs, filling them up, before being released, traveling out of your lungs and out of your body—exhaled into the world. Focus on the way your heart is beating in time with your breathing, and feel how it pumps blood throughout your body.

You can even focus on sounds or smells around you. Maybe there's a bird singing outside your window. Maybe someone recently mowed their lawn, and now everything smells like freshly-cut grass. Focus on the sensation of touch; the way the ground feels beneath your feet, the way the air feels on your skin.

Once you have achieved an awareness of the present, you can slowly begin to reintroduce your awareness of your emotional state. Allow your thoughts to flow through you, and exhale both the air from your lungs and the negative thoughts from your mind.

Watch as these negative thoughts disappear while you remain present in the world, and remember the critical part of self-awareness theory: You are not your thoughts. Your past trauma may have left you with negative thought patterns, but that does not mean those thought patterns represent who you are.

———————◆O◆———————

The way we experience the world is so often determined by how we think about ourselves and life. This is why it's so essential to tame these thoughts, so we can choose how we want to live. With time and a bit of effort, you'll be able to gain awareness of your thoughts, change negative thinking patterns, and live the life you want.

Chapter 3

Emotions

Taking care of your thoughts

*"You don't stop laughing when you grow old,
you grow old when you stop laughing."*
—George Bernard Shaw

T he physical body is the medium through which we can feel emotions. If we were only a spirit, we would not feel anything, neither the butterflies in our stomach, nor the goosebumps; we would not be able to feel the chills down our spine.

It is only through the body that emotions become real. External events generally trigger them, but they are kept alive by our thoughts.

We do not see them, but we feel them. Although emotions are not tangible, they can transform our mood, our way of relating to others, and alter the vision we have of ourselves, along with the world around us.

While it is nearly impossible to control emotions—and I would even call it harmful to try—it is possible to manage our thoughts. You can feel more than one emotion simultaneously, even if they are opposites: Fear and excitement, surprise and happiness, and so on. But you cannot have more than one thought.

The solution of switching our focus from controlling our emotions to managing our thoughts is such a simple formula that it doesn't seem true.

This is the fundamental point to keep in mind, which warns us against the automatic defenses that are put in place to help, but end up trapping us.

When we are overwhelmed by an emotional wave, our reality is altered. As long as this vision is temporary, it does not cause damage, but when it becomes persistent and redundant, we must have the strength to acknowledge it and act to get out of it.

We are not our emotions, nor our thoughts; we are much more.

We have the power to consciously guide what we think. It is neither easy, nor taken for granted. It is a constant and daily job, but we can all do it.

Being Human

There are many emotions, and while they differ in intensity from person to person, the truth is that every person experiences a wide range of them. I think that's important to remember, as it's so easy to forget when caught in your own emotional turmoil that other people have and do feel the same way as you. Emotions are a part of being human, after all! They're an integral part of the human experience and, in many ways, are a thread that binds all of humanity together.

What differs isn't experiencing emotions, but rather, how we experience them. How you think, feel, and react to life and its situations makes up your emotional journey.

The first step in learning how to make the most of your emotions is understanding them. At their most basic level, there are six emotions that, when combined, shape your attitude and behavior towards life. Their overlap gives rise to more complex emotions, and it is for this reason that it can be so often tricky to understand what you are experiencing.

I'll go through these basic emotions, to try and help you understand how to recognize and manage them.

Happiness

Happiness is often the emotion most people work the hardest towards experiencing. The pursuit of happiness is a massive part of our culture, and it can sometimes feel like everywhere you look, someone new is telling you a different secret towards unlocking happiness in your life.

However, this can be so misleading and is one of the reasons many people feel themselves becoming miserable when they search for happiness. We think there is a specific type of happiness that we can achieve by following a particular set of rules. Still, the truth remains that happiness is, just like every emotion, something we all experience differently. For some people, happiness is found in bustling cities, while others find happiness in the quiet of nature.

No matter how you find your happiness, the way you perceive it remains the same. It is a pleasant emotion filled with feelings of joy, gratification, fulfillment, and general well-being.

Many of us express our happiness by smiling, laughing, speaking upbeat, and moving with loose, relaxed body language. When we experience an outburst of joy, we might feel giddy or filled with energy; it's the type of feeling that might make you want to get up and move, even twirling around or dancing!

There are many ways to describe happiness, and not all of these ways mean the same thing. Love, amusement, pride, joy, and relief are all seen as expressions of happiness, but they represent different facets of happiness. When you're talking to others about feeling happy, try to pinpoint the specific expression of this emotion that you're experiencing. This can help you better understand how happiness exists in your life.

When you experience an outburst of happiness, allow yourself to enjoy that sensation. Let yourself smile, and share that happiness with others. Just as negative emotions are almost contagious, so are positive emotions! When you're happy, the people around you will feed off that energy. It's why happy people are said to brighten a room so often.

Many studies have linked happiness to well-being. One study even found a correlation between happiness and longevity (Lawrence et al., 2015). So, next time you feel an outburst of joy, indulge in that feeling and reap the health benefits.

Anger

Anger is a powerful emotion and is often viewed in a negative light. Hostility, agitation, and frustration are all aspects of anger, and this emotion can be triggered by your fight or flight instincts.

Often, anger is misunderstood. While too much anger can be unhealthy, it's not an inherently negative emotion.

Anger is a natural and meaningful response to situations where you face injustices or threats. It is an emotion that swells inside you when you feel mistreated or misrepresented. You feel rage, fury, and resentment when you think you have been "done wrong by."

Anger is sometimes a way to understand if the situation you are in has become toxic. It can help you realize your needs, and teach you how to find out what things cross boundaries, when you may not have even been aware of this crossing beforehand. It's a defense mechanism, and when it gets to the core, anger is a way to protect yourself.

We express anger in many ways. Typically, our hearts beat faster, and our faces grow red. We frown or glare, and our bodies become tense or rigid. Many of us will form fists and, under the onslaught of emotion, will find our voices becoming raised.

It is not easy to express this overwhelming feeling.

While we are angry, it is as if a battle is taking place within us. Our words often become confused, or worse still, they hurt others. But if we repress this emotion, we risk turning it into deep and bitter resentment.

Therefore, we must find what it is that helps us find the balance; a way to vent our anger, let it melt, and then look at it objectively. This is important because while it is essential not to repress it, it is equally important not to hurt anyone in this altered state. After all, every word said or action done can become an arrow. When this arrow is launched in anger, it transforms us into the antagonist of our own stories, plunging us further into this endless cycle of pain.

If you find yourself getting angrier, it's usually a good idea to walk away from the situation. Putting distance between you and what triggered your anger will help you look at the problem from a new perspective. Try going for a walk, listening to music, doing breathing exercises, or talking to a friend.

Attempt to verbalize your feelings. Talking about your anger can help you understand the reason why you're angry. It can also help those around you comprehend your rage.

When talking about anger, something to remember is to express yourself clearly and use unambiguous language. Some words, after all, mean different things to different people. Take the word upset, for example. Some people associate being upset with anger, while others associate being upset with sadness. Using words like frustrated, annoyed, infuriated, irritated, and mad will help clarify your fury.

Sadness

Sadness is an unfortunate part of our emotional reality. At some point, we all feel sadness. It can be incredibly cathartic when it is a transient emotion, as significant expressions of sadness are ways to purge this emotion from our bodies. Crying, for example, while unpleasant at the time, often leaves you feeling better afterward.

Prolonged sadness, however, can become depression. This is why it is essential to feel sadness when it occurs. Much like anger, sadness is not inherently harmful, but can have detrimental effects when not properly managed.

The most common expression of sadness is crying, but feeling exhausted, withdrawing into yourself, and being quiet are all expressions of sorrow. Sometimes sadness can be hard to spot in others and even in yourself, so when you face an event that might bring about sadness, give yourself the space to feel down.

Sadness, like happiness, encompasses an array of emotions. Loneliness, grief, hopelessness, disappointment, and misery are all facets of sorrow. Understanding how you feel sad can help you understand the best way to express, feel, and release your grief.

When you experience an outburst of sadness, the best thing you can do is allow the emotion to run its course. Allow yourself to mourn! Mourning is how we process and cope with loss, and not just loss in the face of death. Breakups, failures, setbacks, and other life situations can all constitute losses and can all be mourned.

Try to do something creative or meaningful. Oftentimes, getting out of your head will help you healthily process your sadness. Finding ways to feel connected to the world around you will help you remember life outside of sadness.

If you genuinely struggle, reaching out to others is also an option. Shared grief is a powerful thing, and there is a reason so many cultures come together when faced with death. Reaching out to those who are not going through the same thing as you can also help, as they can provide a source of comfort and security. Having people to lean on in times of hardship can be a great help in moving forward.

Disgust

Disgust is a visceral emotion. It's a reaction to unpleasant or unwanted things and is often associated with sights, tastes, or smells. Many believe disgust evolved as a way for our ancestors to avoid food that had gone bad, thereby protecting us from food poisoning.

However, disgust isn't limited to physical experiences. There is also moral disgust when we see someone behaving in a way we find distasteful or repulsive. In many ways, disgust is another emotion that protects us from things we should avoid.

Disgust is a visceral emotion. It gives life to phrases like 'skin-crawling' and 'stomach churning.' There is a strong physical reaction to what disgusts us, often demonstrated by turning away from our gagging, wrinkling noses, or even dry-heaving or nausea.

While disgust is meant to protect us from what we find genuinely off-putting, problems can arise when we feel disgusted by things that don't deserve our disgust. One typical example of this is when we grow to feel disgusted by ourselves.

Disgust is characterized as revulsion, loathing, discomfort, and offense. When you think of loathing, consider how often you have seen the term with the self prefix. Self-loathing is one of the most harmful ways disgust can manifest and is one of the ways this emotion can be warped.

When you feel an outburst of disgust, try to remove yourself from the situation bringing you this discomfort. If you can avoid these things, like certain foods or certain sights—a good friend of mine can't watch medical shows because she finds the surgery scenes too stomach churning—then you should do your best to cut these things out of your life.

If, however, you can't avoid what disgusts you, there are a few ways to handle it. During the moment, breathing exercises often help ease overwhelming feelings of repulsion. You can also try to focus on something else; distract your mind, and bring it into a comfortable situation.

Surprise

Surprise is somewhat unique, as it is a neutral emotion. Our responses to the moment of surprise characterize whether it was a positive or negative emotional experience. It's a response to a startling event, piece of information, or circumstance and is typically only felt for an instant.

Shocking events also stick in our minds longer, and it's why surprising things remain in our memories. Stunning upsets in sports games, dramatic performances by entertainers, or shocking twists in movies make the experience more memorable.

Like disgust, there's an actual physical element to surprise. We often cry out, shriek, or even jump. It's like a jolt goes through our systems; our hearts seem to skip a beat, and our jaws typically drop open. Even once the initial shock passes, the effects of the surprise can stay with us, such as by having a racing heart or shaking hands.

This is because surprise often activates the fight or flight adrenaline response. It can leave us prepared to flee, or it can completely stop us in our tracks, leaving us almost dumbfounded. In many ways, we freeze up when we're surprised; our minds needing an extra moment to take in what startled us.

When we are taken by surprise, we may feel embarrassed, perhaps because it happened in public. The key to managing it is to remind ourselves that it happens to everyone.

Laugh at your surprise, especially if it's a harmless joke or prank. Not taking yourself too seriously is a very powerful weapon in certain situations.

If it's something more serious, try to stay calm. The surprise warns us of the situation, but it does not control the situation.

Fear

Fear, like anger, emerges in the face of perceived threats. It is perhaps the most fundamental emotion for survival, as it is a strong indicator of when something is dangerous or wrong. Fear is the emotion that most strongly evokes the fight or flight response and can help you make sure you are ready to face any upcoming threats.

However, it's important to remember that while fear responds to an immediate threat, it can also exist when we feel anxious regarding potential events or situations. This anxiety will magnify the fear response you experience and make you feel a disproportionate amount of fear about your circumstances. If this happens, it's important to remember that while the anxiety you're experiencing is valid, it is also likely somewhat irrational.

Just as is the case with every emotion, there are different levels and experiences of fear. Worry, for example, is a type of lower-level fear, especially when compared to terror. Panic, nervousness, desperation, and horror are all other ways to describe your fear. When communicating this emotion, using the right word can help others understand what you're going through.

If you find yourself grappling with an overwhelming amount of fear, there are a few things you can do to help combat this emotion. Exposure therapy, for example, is used to treat fears. It utilizes the idea that, with familiarity, the situation can become less frightening. While sometimes feeling like the best solution, avoiding your fears will usually wind up making things worse in the long run. Sometimes, facing your fears is the best solution, as hard as that may be.

You can also try to distract yourself when you're experiencing overwhelming fear. High levels of worry and stress can lead you to ruminate on the situation if you have anxiety. This only serves to compound the fear you're experiencing. So, when you find your mind beginning to fall into a fear spiral, practice thought awareness and consciously redirect it towards something comforting.

<hr />

Negative Emotions

Anger, fear, frustration, and disgust are commonly seen as negative emotions. However, they are essential to the human experience, which cannot be complete without them. Very often, though, they contribute to creating stress and anxiety in our life.

For this reason, we probably sometimes tend to avoid facing these emotions; hiding our sadness, repressing our anger, being ashamed of our fear. We try to put them aside, and neglect them until they become part of us.

We must act before this happens.

Ignoring them does not help us, and as difficult as it is, we must understand that, as they are a fundamental part of our journey, the only way is to accept them and learn how to manage them before they do us harm.

The Effects of Negative Emotions

As I said, negative emotions can hurt your health. Numerous studies have shown this to be accurate, both physically and mentally. In terms of physical effects, it has long been known that stress is incredibly damaging. High blood pressure, headaches, poor sleep, and stomach problems are physical symptoms of chronic stress.

Psychologically, negative emotions can significantly harm your mental health. They can lead to upticks in depression and anxiety, and even cause panic attacks. When we allow negative emotions to fester within us, they begin to act like an infection, slowly spreading throughout our bodies and making us sick.

They can even have unexpected effects on your health. One study, conducted on 98 participants, found that those with poor anger control—and therefore, higher levels of anger in their lives—healed from injuries slower than those with reasonable anger control (Gouin et al., 2008).

Negative emotions can affect more than just your health. They have also been shown to affect your relationships with others and yourself. If left unchecked, negative emotions have the potential to destroy relationships. Many people who struggle with managing their anger find themselves almost compelled to ruin relationships.

This is a form of self-sabotage and is common in more than just people who experience difficulties with excessive rage. It's a common habit in anyone who has experienced trauma. Self-sabotage occurs when you decide to ruin something yourself, before someone else can ruin it for you. It's a way of protecting yourself from rejection, betrayal, and other forms of pain. However, it's faulty protection, as it doesn't protect you from any pain at all. It just means that, instead of someone else hurting you, you're hurting yourself.

As you can see, negative emotions can do overwhelming harm. However, they don't have to control you. With a bit of patience, you can learn how to take control back from your negative emotions and manage them in a healthy, positive way.

Emotional Triggers

Emotional triggers are the catalysts to emotional outbursts. They can be anything from a memory, an experience, to even a sound or a scent which could act as a trigger. They can be tough to deal with, especially when you aren't entirely sure about your emotional triggers.

You can usually tell when you're experiencing an overwhelming emotional reaction; your heartbeat races, your breath quickens, your hands clench, your skin flushes. You feel hot or cold, and your mind might even go blank. You might feel shaky, dizzy, or even nauseous.

When you feel this way, listen to your body's reaction and make a note of your surroundings. Try to step back and see if you can determine what brought on such a strong reaction. You might notice a pattern in your responses, and in time you might be able to trace them back to a root cause.

By learning to recognize your emotional triggers, you can learn to cope with them. For some people, this means avoiding certain things. However, that isn't always a viable option. Life is unexpected, after all, and you can't control what everyone else does. Don't worry, though! Instead of avoiding triggers, you can learn how to manage your responses to them using similar techniques that you can employ for thought awareness.

Mindfulness, especially, is an excellent coping technique. It's known to help people learn to process unpleasant feelings better, and processing your emotions is half the battle for emotional management. Meditation, as well, is a great tactic you can employ, as is journaling, especially gratitude journaling. After all, practicing gratitude reminds us of the good in our lives, and this practice can help free us from emotional spirals.

Another technique you could employ is emotional freedom technique (EFT) tapping. EFT tapping builds on acupuncture and treats both physical pain and emotional upset. Utilizing what is known as meridian points throughout your body, EFT tapping helps you balance your energy.

You can divide EFT tapping into five steps. When you're in the middle of an overwhelming onslaught of negative emotions, try this technique to help you regain a sense of calm.

Step One: Identifying the problem. To treat the issue, you must first know what it is. This is why EFT tapping should be used in conjunction with other techniques. Meditation and journaling, for example, are great ways to illuminate the root cause of many issues.

Step Two: Determining intensity. On a scale of 0 to 10, try to determine how much pain you are experiencing. Understanding the pain levels will help you keep track of your progress as you employ this technique. Think of it this way—if your initial pain level is an 8, and you're able to reduce it to a 4, then you've halved your pain.

Step Three: The focal phrase. Before you start tapping, you must understand the cause of your pain and prepare a mantra or affirmation you can say while employing this technique. This focal phrase should address both the problem you're having and your self-acceptance, despite the issue. For example, a phrase like "Though I am afraid, I wholly accept myself."

Step Four: The tapping sequence. Once you've settled on your phrase, it's time to start tapping. EFT tapping uses nine meridian points. In order of tapping, these points are as follows: The fleshy part of your outer hand, eyebrow, side of the eye, under the eye, under the nose, the chin, the beginning of the collarbone, under the armpit on the lateral side of the chest, and on the top of the head. The technique is done only on one part of the body, and it is indifferent whether on the right or left side.

When tapping, the sequence begins with the fleshy part of the outer hand. This is known as the karate chop meridian. Tap this point as you recite your focal sentence a few times. Once this is done, move on to the next seven meridians. Tap each of these points at least seven or eight times before moving on to the next one. After you are done tapping under the arm, complete the sequence by tapping the top of the head.

During this sequence, be sure to focus on your problem area. Remind yourself of your focal phrase, and remember that you can rise above your pain. Repeat this sequence at least two to three times, or as many times as you feel you need.

Step Five: Re-examining intensity. After you have completed each sequence, re-examine your pain. If it is not entirely gone, repeat the sequence. Checking in with yourself can help you understand your pain and potentially re-evaluate your initial assessment of your pain levels.

It is advisable to follow the entire sequence when you are in a quiet place without possible interruptions, but when I need to do it urgently and quickly (maybe out of sudden anger or anxiety), I only focus on 2/3 points (for example hand, armpit, head). Trying it costs nothing, but I assure you that if you are consistent with this, you will find it effective.

Caring for Your Emotions

Being emotionally healthy is essential to living a happy and fulfilling life. However, that doesn't mean you must be happy all the time! Being emotionally healthy means learning to be self-aware and managing your emotions. It means taking care of your feelings and learning to respect them, even those you don't necessarily enjoy.

Caring for your emotions is critical to emotional wellness. As we learn to accept our feelings, we also understand them and foster empathy for both our feelings and ourselves. In many ways, working on your emotional health will also help you learn to accept who you are and what you have experienced.

Your emotional health doesn't only affect your mental or physical well-being. It can play a part in your relationships, career, and in many other aspects. Since we experience emotions in every walk of life, it only makes sense that emotional wellness affects every part of our being.

There are many ways to work on your emotional well-being. Practicing gratitude is one of them, as is being respectful towards yourself and others. Taking the time to engage in self-care and learning to love yourself will also play a massive role in improving your emotional health. Exercise, meditation, mindfulness, and journaling are excellent ways to work on this.

However, all of these techniques fall under the umbrella of living a balanced life. A balanced lifestyle makes time for work, friends, family, and yourself. It means sleeping well, eating well, and exercising. It can sound impossible, but you don't have to do everything each day!

Cramming everything into a single day doesn't make for a balanced life; that's a recipe for an exhausting one. Try to set up routines that focus on the long-term, rather than the short-term. Check-in with yourself, and see if you feel you have been neglecting any areas of your life. Focus on engaging in activities and relationships that make you happy and that you genuinely enjoy.

<hr />

Emotional wellness is a personal journey. If you find that specific techniques aren't working for you the way they might for other people, that isn't a failure. It just means that you have different needs. Try different strategies, techniques, and lifestyle changes to find what works for you. When you enjoy doing something, you're more likely to do it, and that's what you want when it comes to promoting emotional wellness.

Chapter 4

Resilience

Answering the pain points

"Change is the law of life. And those who look only to the past or present are certain to miss the future."
—John F. Kennedy

"Do not judge me by my success, judge me by how many times I fell down and got back up again."
◻ Nelson Mandela

I t's unpleasant, looking at a wound. They can be raw, gaping, and unbearably painful. It isn't so easy to avoid looking at physical injuries, though. They stand in plain sight. However, the wounds born of trauma are all too easy to avoid. They bring you pain, but you convince yourself that if you don't look, they can't hurt you.

The problem is that until you look upon the wounds from your trauma—until you confront these wounds, and truly face them head-on—you can't begin to focus on what brings you peace. If it's your past that haunts you, then the pain is rooted in the memories of your past.

It's challenging to overcome past hardships—I know that well—but I can promise you that you can move on, so long as you choose to do so. So make that choice! Find out the possibilities in front of you and examine them.

I'll be honest, one of the choices you can make is to continue your suffering; to live on as you have been, with still-bleeding wounds. But the alternatives are so much more than that. There are endless possibilities, and you just have to choose which path to follow.

Traumas of the Future Past

Traumas of the future past might sound like a science fiction movie, but I assure you, that's not the case. This refers to something in the past that still affects you, like a thorn under your foot, digging into your skin.

Trauma is that thorn. It lingers inside you and hurts you for years, often in ways you don't even realize. It damages relationships, your health, your career, and even your hobbies. Trauma can cause mental illnesses like depression and anxiety, and it's known that people with depression stop engaging in the things they love.

It's difficult to know how to process trauma. Many of us blame ourselves for what happened, which leads to overwhelming feelings of guilt and shame. That shame then sticks with you throughout the rest of your life, and it can affect the way you learn to connect and interact with other people.

Some people with trauma may withdraw, building walls around themselves and avoiding attachments. From the outside, they might appear independent and self-sufficient. Inside, though, they are cutting themselves off as a protective mechanism, keeping themselves from experiencing the pain that past trauma has brought them.

Other people may seek external validation, even crave it, and constantly seek it out in their relationships. They might seem overly attached or clingy, searching for the emotional stability and assurance they might never have received.

Others, still, might always have their guard up. They seem disconnected and are never entirely able to trust other people. In response to having been hurt before, they begin to think that everyone will hurt them in that same way. These people might appear cold or aloof, when in reality, they are struggling to find a way to trust again.

As you can see, trauma affects people in different ways. People display trauma with varying signs depending on their personality, the type of trauma they have experienced, and other internal and external factors.

Signs of Emotional Baggage

It's easy to look at people and miss the signs in their behaviors that indicate they are struggling with past baggage and trauma. It's also easy not to realize signs of emotional baggage within yourself. If you've lived with this baggage for a while, you might mistake certain behaviors as being a part of your personality.

A typical example of this is people who experience anxiety due to trauma, particularly social anxiety. You might consider yourself a shy and reserved person, tending towards introversion. However, this could be a result of trauma. After treating their anxiety, some people find themselves outgoing and no longer shy. It wasn't their personality that made them reserved; it resulted from their emotional baggage.

Anxiety and depression are common effects of past trauma. In addition to these, you might also find yourself exhausted all the time and struggling with low self-esteem. This exhaustion and lack of confidence can manifest as symptoms of anxiety or depression, but they can also display on their own.

Low self-esteem can present itself in a few ways; you might be overly critical towards yourself, you might feel uncomfortable in your own skin, or you might struggle with standing up for yourself.

You can trace many of these feelings back to guilt and shame. If you feel as though what happened to you was your fault—as though you in some way deserved it—and you begin to believe that every misfortune you experience from that point on is also deserved, this will lead to a devaluing of yourself and contribute to feelings of worthlessness.

Exhaustion occurs because we only have so much energy to handle life each day. If there is a large portion of your emotional energy dedicated to your trauma, you're going to run out of energy faster than other people.

On the flip side of exhaustion is apathy. To preserve their energy, some people grow desensitized from the world around them. This can lead to depersonalization or derealization; the feeling that you are detached from the world around you. For some people, that can feel like they aren't in their bodies. For others, it can feel as though they're watching the world through a glass window.

Self-destructive behavior is another sign you might be carrying emotional baggage. Activities like smoking, drinking, binge eating, or engaging in reckless activities like gambling, are examples of self-destructive behaviors. These can be a way to escape intrusive thoughts or numb pain for some. For others, these activities can be a way to punish oneself.

Hopelessness about the future is another way to tell if you're carrying trauma. You believe that good things won't happen for you, and you always expect adverse outcomes. You might not be able to think that any relationship will last, and you might even believe that certain life milestones won't happen for you.

These are only some of the potential signs that you might have emotional baggage. Others include difficulties forming healthy attachments or struggling with emotional regulation. When you find yourself experiencing any of these behaviors or responses, try to practice mindfulness, thought awareness, EFT tapping, or other coping strategies I've discussed.

Remember, as well, that these responses don't have to control you. Past trauma is tough to move on from. Our brains cling to negativity, and it's so much easier to see the dark side than it is to see the light one. Trauma has a way of shaping us, but you don't have to let it continue to do so.

More than that, we grow used to the pain. We are comfortable with familiar territory and sticking to what we know, even when it hurts us. Letting go of that known ground and forging ahead into an unknown future is neither easy, nor a step that should be taken for granted.

You might not see a future for yourself, but there is one. After all, even when the sun sets, we know it will be back again tomorrow. Remember that just because you're in the dark, that doesn't mean you will never again stand in the light.

By working through your pain, you will realize a new version of yourself; a positive self, which can make room for new opportunities for happiness. You will gain the strength that comes from overcoming pain, and you might even find that your story helps other people who have gone through similar things.

What Has Happened Has Happened

The truth is, holding on to the past is just as much a conscious choice as letting it go. Whatever path you take, it is a path you choose. The problem is that it is easy to hold on to the past. It is much more challenging to let go. However, it is also one of the most rewarding and life-affirming choices you can make.

It's also a choice that you must make, over and over. You can't expect overnight change; you won't wake up one morning magically healed with a perfect dream-like life. You have to put in work, choosing every day to continue forward with your decision to leave the past behind. You must choose, again and again, to work towards building a better present and future for yourself.

Instead of thinking about how things could have gone or the life you should have had, focus on the lessons you have learned. Your life isn't over yet. There's still time to have a happy, healthy, joyful life.

I'll go over a few strategies you can use to let go of your pain and live that better life:

Positive Mantra

The way you speak to yourself can considerably affect your ability to move forwards. Just like with affirmations, using negative language can do more harm than good. When you're experiencing emotional pain, try not to think in terms of "why did this happen to me," or "I can't believe I had to go through that."

Instead, focus on uplifting and empowering language. This will help reframe your thoughts and help get you free from negativity spirals. Try to say something like "I am strong and capable and have survived," or "I feel blessed that I can start down a new, healthy path in life."

Physical Distance

It isn't running away—it's removing yourself from a bad situation. It's easy to believe that creating physical distance between you and what hurt you is akin to fleeing, to giving up and hiding, but that isn't true at all. Having space between you and the source of your pain will help you begin to let go. Without the chance of re-encountering the catalyst of your pain, you're more likely to not constantly worry about it. Out of sight, out of mind, after all!

Focus on Yourself

This is essential to letting go of your pain. At the beginning of the chapter, I told you that you must face your pain to move past it. While that's true, it's also something that can be easily misconstrued. When looking your trauma in the face, remember to not focus on the person or situation that hurt you. Instead, you have to look at yourself.

Focusing on yourself doesn't only apply when facing your pain. It also applies to practicing mindfulness. I've said it before, and I'll say it again—practicing mindfulness is one of the best things you can do for your mental, emotional, spiritual, and physical health!

When you catch yourself ruminating on your pain, pull your thoughts back to the present and focus on yourself. What you are feeling, what you are doing, how the ground feels beneath your feet, how a warm cup of tea feels cupped between your hands—whatever it is, ground yourself in the moment and remember your blessings.

Practice Self-Kindness

You have to be kind to yourself. I can't repeat that enough: You have to be kind to yourself. We're trained to be self-critical, constantly doubt ourselves, and pick at our faults. Every misstep feels like a failure of the largest magnitude.

Instead of being critical towards yourself, try to be compassionate. Grant yourself grace for the moments you feel you fall short; the same way you would for your loved ones. Try to treat yourself the way you would treat your friends.

Being kind to yourself encompasses more aspects than you might think. Self-care is an act of self-love and self-compassion. Doing nice things for yourself, taking time to relax, and caring for your needs are all ways you can engage in self-kindness.

When you are in pain and hurting, choose to treat yourself with kindness rather than harshness. Redirect your thoughts from negative self-talk to more forgiving alternatives. Learning to love yourself is a long journey, but it starts with the simple act of self-kindness.

Express Anger in a Safe Way

It's easy to be afraid of anger. It feels aggressive, primal even, and can cloud your judgment. However, it's important to remember that anger and aggression are not the same thing. Expressing your anger doesn't mean getting physical or lashing out. It means allowing the anger to flow through you, listening to the anger, understanding it, and releasing it through healthy means.

That could be journaling, painting, exercising, or playing an instrument. Even listening to music can help. All of these are healthy and safe ways you can express your anger.

Practice Forgiveness

One of the most difficult things to practice is forgiveness, because while it's easy to put forgiveness into words, it is challenging to feel it with the heart.

A phrase that I find incredibly incoherent is "I forgive, but I do not forget" because it is a fundamental contradiction. How can we forgive if we continue to remember a memory that causes us pain?

The pain comes from the fact that we feel that an injustice has been done to us, and it is difficult to accept that it is dismissed without consequences, as it has left us with wounds.

Sometimes we conflate forgiveness with absolution, as if we were sending the implicit message that what the other person did was acceptable. When we do this, we are, in some way, absolving them of blame.

Starting from the fact that to feel free, we must also let go of resentment; how can we forgive if we continue to feel the sense of injustice in this act?

The key is to change the way you think about forgiveness.

Rather than an act of absolution, try to look at forgiveness as an act of acceptance. You accept what has happened to you and you have learned to let go. Think of forgiveness as the act of acknowledging that what has happened has happened. Think of it as a way to let go of the fear, anger, shame, and guilt that has been weighing you down and causing you pain. Forgiveness is an act of letting go of what has hurt you, after all. There's no apology needed for that.

⸺⸺◆O◆⸺⸺

Remember, though, that these strategies are not the be-all and end-all of letting go of your pain. Don't be afraid to seek professional help if you find yourself struggling. It can be hard to process things on your own, so speaking with a trained professional might be what you need.

Once you've decided to move forward and have incorporated these strategies into your life, I promise that you'll see a difference. It's the weight on your shoulders; you might not know it's there, but as soon as it's lifted, you'll feel lighter, happier. By addressing your pain, you'll be able to see peace.

Chapter 5

Self-Love

Be compassionate with yourself

"You find peace not by rearranging the circumstances of your life but by realizing who you are at the deepest level."
—Eckhart Tolle

E ven now, there are still many people who think of self-love as a hoax. They see it as some overblown theory, and even if they choose to engage with self-love, they don't go further than reading a handful of self-help books or watching a few YouTube videos on the matter. They don't truly take the time to practice self-love, and so they never grow to understand all of its benefits.

Self-love is so much more than so many people think! It's a critical practice that can bring your life blessings in various ways. I'll go over the importance of self-love, as well as some powerful strategies you can employ to foster self-love in your life. By the time I'm finished, you'll see just how extraordinary self-love truly is.

———◆◇◆———

The Importance of Self-Love

One of the worst things the world has done for our psyches is try to convince us that the pursuit of perfection is worthwhile. We chase perfectionism, being inundated with people telling us to work hard, and then we work harder, so we can be successful.

Have you ever wondered why you have to work so hard to succeed? Why can't we work blissfully to find success? This is a large part of the perfectionism problem. There is, after all, no such thing as being perfect. It's a losing battle, no matter how hard you work.

When you use perfectionism as a motivator, you aren't helping yourself. Rather, you're actively harming yourself. The pursuit of perfection inspires self-criticism and self-flagellation, as you constantly fall short of the impossible standards you've set. You always believe that, even when you've done well, you could have done better. Nothing you do can ever be good enough when you adopt this mindset.

More than that, perfectionism takes a toll on your physical health. As it can lead to greater stress levels in your life, it's been linked to heart problems, depression, gut problems, and even a shorter lifespan.

How, then, can you combat perfectionism? The answer lies in the opposite of perfectionism's self-critical mindset. That is, in the practice of self-love. A study published in 2018 found that practicing self-compassion undermines the effects of toxic perfectionism and self-criticism (Ferrari et al., 2018).

Self-love can combat the effects of perfectionism by the simple fact of its existence. Self-love entails being kind to yourself, practicing mindfulness, and understanding that you are human and humans make mistakes.

Loving yourself isn't about being a narcissist either, which is a common misconception. It's about granting yourself room to make mistakes without fear of being berated. It's about forgiving yourself when you fall short, as you accept the different things that make you who you are. Self-love is about acknowledging your true self and embracing it wholeheartedly.

Beyond combating perfectionism, self-love is essential for other reasons, too! It can boost your self-confidence, reduce stress in your life, and help you find your happiness. By ridding yourself of the critical inner voice that tears you down, you will find room to grow into the strong and resilient person you have always been at your core.

Self-love is also the first step to creating more meaningful and healthy relationships. When you love yourself, you can be secure in the love of others. When you're plagued by self-doubt and self-hatred, you convince yourself that someone loving you is a lie. You may even think you're deceiving people into loving you. Self-love, however, shows you that this is not the case.

When you practice self-love, you will find it helps you see what your loved ones see in you. It shows you that you're a beautiful being deserving of love, just as you are. You don't have to do anything special to earn a life of light and happiness. You deserve that by simply existing in this world.

Self-love can also help you learn to overcome your past. Past trauma and hardships can lead you to believe that you're worth less than you are. Cultivating self-compassion means deriving your worth from internal sources, not external. In overcoming your past pain, you begin to see that what happened to you is not who you are. You understand that you are so much more than your pain. This helps us move past negative experiences, as we can see who we truly are.

At its core, self-love is about building a loving and healthy relationship with yourself. Healthy relationships are built on trust, compassion, and respect. As you practice self-love, you will learn to apply those traits inwards. While practicing self-love is, at first, something you must consciously do, it will become a reflex over time, replacing criticism and doubt as your knee-jerk response to situations.

A Prescription to Loving Yourself

As you can see, indulging in self-love is a no-brainer. You have every right and possibility to live happily and take care of yourself. It's not foolish, selfish, or narcissistic to love yourself. In truth, it's the best possible thing you could do for yourself. Here are a few tricks and strategies you can employ in your life to practice self-love:

Don't Compare Yourself to Someone Else

Humans are competitive by nature. It's why we love competitions so much, from sporting events to talent shows. While there's nothing inherently wrong with being competitive, the issue arises when we treat everyone and everything as a competition. For women especially, we are often socialized to treat each other as rivals for job opportunities, friendships, and love, to name a few.

When you look at the world and only see opponents, you fall into the trap of constantly comparing yourself to the people you see around you.

We are bombarded daily with prototypes that are impossible to reach: In newspapers, on TV, and on social media. This confrontation undermines our self-confidence.

Have you ever felt a sense of inadequacy, or of not being worthy? Has this come about by comparing yourself with the perfect bodies, or with the successes achieved by strangers you find on social media?

Although we rationally know that the perfection and success we assign to others may not always be true, it still triggers a comparison that leads us to be particularly critical of ourselves. It feeds into our self-doubt and toxic perfectionism, making it hard to remember to practice self-love.

Remember, though, that it's useless to compare yourself to someone else! After all, you're you, and they're them—that is to say, everyone is different. We achieve different things at different times, and that's perfectly fine! When you learn to focus on your journey in life, rather than the journey of others, you'll feel lighter and happier.

Don't Let the Opinions of Others Affect You

When you focus too much on what other people think of you, you forget to pay attention to what you feel about yourself. Don't let society's standards for how your life should look keep you from happiness. After all, what is suitable for someone else might not be right for you.

Think of it this way: There are different styles in art, but not everyone appreciates them equally. Some may love minimalism, and others may prefer hyperrealism. Some love modern and conceptual art; others, the Renaissance period. As much as one can love art, it is impossible that a work of art can absolutely please everyone or equally impact each person. It wouldn't be art if it did.

If this can be understood, why can't we accept that everything else in life follows the same logic?

Consider yourself a unique and unrepeatable work of art. You can never please everyone, and whatever you do, there will always be someone who will have a critical opinion. So at this point, try to be the person you want to be, and love who you are. This does not mean being perfect, but accepting yourself with strengths and weaknesses. After all, these characteristics are what make you unique.

Set Boundaries

Setting boundaries is a vital part of self-love. It's an unfortunate fact of life that if you don't have boundaries, there will always be some people who take advantage of you. Setting boundaries is an act of self-respect. When you set boundaries, you stand up for yourself and refuse to engage in work, relationships, and other activities that harm you.

It can be hard to learn how to set boundaries, especially if you aren't entirely sure what those boundaries are. If this is the case for you, try to start with something small and practice saying no. In time, you should expand your boundaries until you find the edge of them. When you reach that point, you'll have plenty of practice standing up for yourself and will have a better sense of self!

Give Yourself Space to Make Mistakes

It's so hard to make mistakes, especially if you struggle with perfectionism. It can feel like a failure and can fill you with self-recriminations. You begin to think of yourself as only your mistakes and grow blind to your successes. This only feeds into the cycle of negativity, though.

You should remember that mistakes are lessons! No one has lived a perfect life; no one has ever lived without making mistakes. It's only natural that we falter from time to time. When that happens, take the opportunity to reflect on the situation and see what you can do differently in the future, rather than beating yourself up. When you begin to do this, you'll stop doubting yourself and start believing in your power!

Let Go of Toxic People

I've said it before, and I'll say it again: Negative people will only bring you down. We're social creatures, and we feed off the energy of others. If you feel worse every time you spend time with someone, that's probably not someone you want to keep in your life.

The people you surround yourself with should empower you, not drag you down. If someone is bringing negativity and toxic energy into your life and isn't trying to change, you shouldn't be afraid to take a step back from that person. It isn't wrong to cut out people who are hurting you!

Listen to Yourself

This pairs well with mindfulness and meditation, as these practices are centered around fostering a deeper connection with your inner self. It's vital to forge and foster this connection, as it can help you understand the difference between what you want and what you need.

While it isn't wrong to go after what you want in life—in fact, I highly encourage you to do so—it's essential to make sure that what you want won't hurt you. When we neglect what we need in favor of what we want, we're bringing harm to ourselves. It's a deep form of self-love when we can turn down exciting or thrilling things that we might want to do, to prioritize our needs instead.

However, these two things don't need to stand in conflict with each other! The more you practice mindfulness, meditation, and self-love, the more you'll find your wants and needs aligning.

Listening to yourself also means learning to trust yourself. It's common to doubt your abilities and worry over whether or not you're making the right decision. Remember, though, that you know yourself best. While your worries are valid—just as all your feelings are—don't let them consume you. Trust your instincts and know that, even if you do make a mistake, it isn't the end of the world.

Take Charge of Your Life

When you live with purpose, you will love yourself more. That doesn't mean you have to find your life's purpose—that's a question philosophers have long struggled with, after all—it means that you have to live intentionally. Set goals for yourself, move with direction, and guide yourself towards outcomes you want to see.

Visualization

There are a few ways you can learn to live with intention. One of these is through a practice known as visualization. Much like using positive affirmations, visualization rewires your brain. It uses the power of your mind to make things happen.

It's been shown that our brains can't always tell the difference between memories and visions of the future. Using that logic, visualization has us envision the outcome we want. Our brains, then, interpret that as a memory, making it easier for us to achieve it—after all, according to our brains, we already have achieved that outcome!

To rewire your brain and practice visualization, you have to stick with it for at least six weeks, being sure to spend between five and ten minutes each day visualizing. You can do this at any time of the day, be it right when you wake up, right before bed, or any time in between.

Try to visualize a specific goal. This will help you have focus and clarity when you begin this practice. If you aren't sure of a goal, ask yourself a few questions, such as, "what is my passion?" or "what are my unique skills and talents?" This can help you find direction.

When you visualize, try to imagine a specific scenario. If you have a job interview coming up, imagine yourself in that interview. Picture yourself, in your mind, confidently answering questions. Imagine the interviewer thanking you and offering you a job or a follow-up interview.

Focus on this image, over and over. Write a reminder of what you would like to achieve and read it every morning. Carry that reminder with you throughout the day to look at when you begin to feel doubts. In time, you will feel confident and more than capable of achieving your goals.

Micro-Planning

Another way you can take charge of your life is by making a plan. Creating a plan drastically reduces stress, and it's one of the best ways to do it, particularly regarding anxieties surrounding our future. Having a plan means having goals, as well as having things we can work towards. This greatly helps us live with purpose and forward momentum as we move through life.

While it might seem impossible to make plans, specifically large overarching ones, since you don't know what the world might throw your way next, you can still engage in a practice known as micro-planning. This is when you take a larger goal or vision and break it down into smaller, more achievable pieces.

This practice gives us a sense of constantly making progress, reducing stress, and propelling us forward. There are six key elements to consider when making a micro-plan of your own.

The first step is to identify your purpose. Why are you making this plan? What is your overall goal? Take time to reflect on this and come up with an answer that feels right to you. Remember, this overall goal will remain the same throughout your planning. While the smaller portions of your plan can be more flexible, this goal should be firm.

Next, you'll need to make a year-long plan. Reflect on the year you're having, and look at where you are now, compared to where you were in the past, and where you would like to be. See what has worked for you, as well as what hasn't, and use those to create your plan. Look for areas of growth you can work on, but don't include too many. Keeping it between one and three will keep you from being overwhelmed.

Step three is to break your year down into quarters, which are each composed of three months. Use the end of each of these quarters to see where you are, regarding both your goal and your plan. If you need to readjust certain things, this is the time to do so.

The next step is to break your plan down, even further, into individual months. You can use each month as a benchmark to achieve smaller goals or to finish any projects you have been working on. Each month can be considered a different step or phase in your process.

You guessed it! The fifth step is weeks. Having weekly tasks means you'll be able to finish what you need, without being stressed out by long to-do lists each day. This is a great way to practice prioritization, as well. Learning which tasks need to be done earlier in the week versus what you can hold off on finishing will help you practice managing your time.

Finally, the sixth step is daily tasks. This typically includes keeping track of how you feel each day. Monitor your energy levels and emotional state, and see when or if you felt overwhelmed. This can help you adjust your plan to suit your needs better.

Embrace Kindness

Be kind to yourself and those around you! When we choose to live in kindness, we begin to radiate positivity. Self-kindness means treating yourself the way you would treat your loved ones. Living in kindness means extending kindness to the people around you, yourself, and everyone else you might encounter.

Celebrate yourself! Celebrate others! Try to see the good that still exists in this world and learn to embrace it wholeheartedly. Mindfulness and practicing gratitude go hand in hand with this aspect of self-love, as both of these focus on remembering the blessings you have in your life and learning to cherish them.

You become more likely to receive kindness in return, when you are kind. When you are kind to yourself, you learn to embrace all the parts of you, even the ones you have struggled to accept. Forgiving yourself and practicing self-respect are both facets of learning to live in kindness.

Take Care of Yourself

Remember to take care of yourself! Practice self-care and make time to engage in activities that bring you joy. Chase your happiness, and allow that happiness to take root within you. The more you prioritize your well-being, the more you will grow to love who you are.

Taking care of yourself is more than just doing fun hobbies; it also includes eating well, exercising regularly, and taking care of your mental health. Yoga is an excellent example of this. Not only is it an excellent workout, but it's also a type of meditation. As you move from stretch to stretch, you focus on your breathing, and feel how your muscles stretch and support you. It gives you a chance to be centered in the moment; learning to exist as one with your body.

Taking care of yourself also means putting yourself first. That can be challenging, especially for women, as we're taught to be self-sacrificing. While it's fine to put others first from time to time, you run into problems when you forget to stop. Taking care of others shouldn't mean sacrificing your well-being.

If you need to take a step back, you should do so. It isn't selfish to take care of yourself. Besides, if there are people who need your help, consider that you can't help them if you aren't taking care of yourself.

Embrace Your Strengths and Weaknesses

Learning to embrace both your strengths and your weaknesses is essential to self-love. It's easy to love your strengths while, at the same time, hating yourself for your shortcomings. However, that isn't love.

Embracing your weaknesses doesn't mean never trying to improve upon them. It means accepting them as a part of you and understanding that being weak doesn't mean you aren't worth love, compassion, and respect. Having weaknesses doesn't mean you're weak, either. It just means you're better at some things than you are at others, and that's true of everyone in the world.

Embrace every part of you, because that's what each is—a part of you. Everything that makes you who you are is worth loving, even the parts you struggle with. Hone your strengths, work on your weaknesses, and take pride in who you are.

———————————◄○►———————————

Self-love is not selfish. Instead, it's the most essential thing you need to do to stay happy and sane in this overwhelming world. Self-love protects you from conflicts, both inner and outer, cushioning you when you fall and carrying you when you falter. Self-love is what will keep you going, bolstering your mind and body to bring you into all the possibilities of the future.

Chapter 6

Self-esteem

Breaking free from self-pity by recognizing your worth

> "Self-pity comes so naturally to us. The most solid happiness can be shaken by the compassion of a fool."
> —*Andre Maurois*

When something goes wrong, people fall into patterns of self-pity. They keep mentally poking at whatever it was that went wrong, looking for answers. While their intentions are usually to eliminate their pain, this over-analyzing only makes things worse. Their heads grow heavy with the weight of the pain, and they use up their mental energy on futile overthinking.

This is what happens when we engage in self-pity. We ruminate, keeping ourselves trapped in the memories of our trauma, lamenting the pain it has caused us.

Since it can tear down our progress, we must guard ourselves against the trap of self-pity. To break free of this habit, we must make a mental shift and break the vicious cycle. This is the only way we can win back control of our lives.

The Self-Pity Enigma

Unfortunately, it becomes easy to fall into the trap of self-pity when something painful and unexpected happens to us. Finding no other answers, we almost come to console ourselves by finding a justification in the fact that what we are going through is due to bad luck; to have everything and everyone against us, and to be alone and defenseless.

We try to find something outside of us that confirms that there was nothing more we could do, and we feel weak in the face of events.

When we are trapped in self-pity, it is difficult to see a way out. Everything becomes monumental, even the smallest fact or action turns into an insurmountable problem. Our energy is slowly devoured.

This is why it is so dangerous.

It's important to note that sadness and self-pity are not the same. While it's normal and sometimes even healthy to experience sadness, feeling self-pity is in no way good for you. While sadness can help us navigate loss and learn to let go of grief, self-pity offers no catharsis. Instead, it keeps us locked in an insidious cycle of hopelessness.

So, what causes self-pity? Often, it's stress that brings about these feelings. When you find yourself grappling with overwhelming anxiety, you might begin to catastrophize.

You imagine the worst possible outcome and convince yourself that it is the only possible outcome. You begin to feel that there is nothing that can be done and that you're beyond help. This feeds into the feelings of hopelessness that often go hand in hand with self-pity.

Anger is another trigger that can lead to feelings of self-pity, especially if you have experienced past pain. As I mentioned, trauma goes hand in hand with feelings of guilt. When you believe you are to blame for your pain, you might find yourself directing your anger inward.

This means that whenever you falter, you blame yourself. This self-blame brings on feelings of helplessness, as though nothing you do is ever good enough. Once again, this traps you in self-pity.

Loneliness, too, can bring about these feelings. More and more, we are acknowledging the emotional toll loneliness takes on people. There's a difference between being lonely and being alone. Being alone can be healthy, as it gives you time to connect with yourself and decompress. Being lonely, however, eats you up.

Self-pity leads us to blame everything by looking outward, losing sight of the goal. If we transform the events—especially the hard and negative ones—into an opportunity for growth, and in the possibility of knowing ourselves in a deeper way, we will discover that we are able to do much more than we previously thought.

Self-Pity in Women

Women are especially vulnerable to the trap of self-pity. This is because women are harder on themselves than men. Women consistently rate themselves lower, are more likely to experience anxiety and depression, are less confident, and are more likely to be overly self-critical than men are, according to psychologists.

But this must not be a justification for indulging in self-pity. Entering the vortex of victimhood does nothing but distance us even further from what we want to achieve, and does not bring about any advantage.

What can we do to change victimized thinking? How can we silence the insinuating voice that, like the annoying dripping of a leaky faucet, continues to whisper in the background of our thoughts, keeping us immobile?

Many people might think self-confidence is the key to overcoming self-pity. After all, wouldn't it be easier to overcome feelings of hopelessness if we're confident in ourselves and our capabilities? While there's truth to that, the problem is that self-pity drains our self-esteem.

We don't act because self-pity undermines the foundation of self-esteem. We feel trapped, but we find no motivation that allows us to stop this spiral and we lose hope of being able to get out of it.

Acceptance and self-love are the first steps towards healing. Accept that we and others can make mistakes, that events can be a way to evolve, and that what happens today can reverse tomorrow.

Self-love focuses on the idea of being kind to yourself. When you practice self-love, you forgive your faults, take care of your needs, and learn to embrace even your weaknesses. By practicing self-love, you directly combat the parts of your mind that self-pity feeds on, thereby giving you the tools to free yourself from its chains.

Finally, above all, you must act. Start with small changes, and don't let yourself be defined by events, as even physical action sets our thoughts in motion and allows us to see things from a different perspective.

Life is like a flowing river. Water can cross countless obstacles, but it is full of life only if it flows, as when it is still, it becomes a muddy swamp.

Self-Pity Isn't Pretty—Get Over It!

Life is too short to spend so much time feeling sorry for yourself. While feeling down from time to time is perfectly normal and sometimes healthy, it should never become a way of life. There's so much good out there waiting for you, so don't miss out on it by trapping yourself in a downwards spiral.

While self-love is a powerful force to use against self-pity, I've put together some more tips and tricks you can use to overcome these feelings.

Be Compassionate

This one is, in many ways, similar to practicing self-love. Being compassionate towards yourself and others, however, is more than that. It's about empathy; about connecting with your emotions the way you would connect to the feelings of others. Look at yourself with kindness and understanding, especially when you're going through a hard time. Extend the same grace to yourself that you would toward your loved ones.

Be compassionate to others, as well. Often, reaching out and connecting with those around you in a healthy, loving way can significantly improve your mental state. When we engage in kindness, compassion, and generosity, we enter into a positive feedback loop. That is, the more compassionate we are, the happier we feel. So next time you find yourself feeling down, try engaging in acts of kindness.

Change Your Perspective

A shift in perspective is one of the most powerful things you can do to change a lot of situations in life. Since self-pity is a mindset, you should try practicing thought awareness and consciously redirect your focus to break away from negative thoughts.

A victim mentality is one of the many reasons you might fall into self-pitying thoughts and behaviors. When you see yourself as a victim, you convince yourself that you are always a victim. This feeds into feelings of helplessness and hopelessness, which are precisely what self-pity uses to keep you trapped. By refusing to be a victim, you take a stand against these negative thoughts, and take control of your life and story.

Another way you can shift your perspective is to challenge your negative thoughts. When you question your perceptions, you actively begin to see how self-pity doesn't hold up to scrutiny. It becomes clear that this negative cycle's worldview isn't realistic.

If you find yourself questioning why bad things always happen to you, challenge that. Think back on the times when good things happened. You'll see that this mindset is inherently wrong by that simple act.

Another great way to change your perspective is to take control of the questions you ask yourself. So often, when we're trapped in ruminations, we ask things like, "why did this happen to me?"

When you ask yourself an open-ended question such as that, it's all too easy for the guilt and shame and self-criticism born of your past pain to slip in and provide false answers. You might tell yourself that you deserved what happened and, instead of thinking about it more, you accept that answer at face value.

Try to ask yourself more productive questions. Instead of "why did this happen to me," try to ask yourself something like, "what could I have done differently?" or "what can I do now?" This takes control back from external factors and returns it to your hands. It also reminds you that, even if you made a mistake, you can learn from it and do things differently in the future.

It's this shift in mentality, from being persecuted to being in control, that helps you escape from negative self-talk and self-doubt. This is a powerful way you can combat feelings of helplessness; you remind yourself that you are the one in control of your life, not anyone or anything else.

Pay Attention to the Pain

When your sadness begins to turn to self-pity, it's essential to sit up and take note of what is happening. While it's hard to catch negative thoughts as they happen, thought awareness trains you in this endeavor, making it easier to recognize the signs that you are entering a negative thinking spiral.

Pay attention to the pain that accompanies self-pity. It isn't only pain directed towards yourself, either. Engaging in self-pity can bring pain to those around you, as your loved ones watch you sink deeper into your trauma. The more negative you are, the worse you become to spend time with. If you struggle to identify your pain, try to watch for pain in others. It's an excellent way to recognize how your self-pity can hurt more than just you.

Try to take action when you notice yourself slipping into self-pity. Listen to yourself, pay attention to your needs, and take action to do something about them. Even when you're feeling down, inactivity can make things worse. It doesn't have to be anything strenuous, either. Meditation, mindfulness, and reflection are all ways you can acknowledge your feelings and start to change your mindset.

Embrace the Good in Your Life

When you feel sorry for yourself, you take on an inherently negative outlook. You focus on the bad rather than the good, with your mind running through all your mistakes and misfortunes. When you ruminate on your pain, you become subsumed by that pain.

Practicing gratitude directly combats this. When you practice gratitude, you constantly remind yourself of all the good in your life. With that much focus on your blessings, a self-pitying mindset can't hold up its facade, and your default state of mind shifts from cynicism to optimism. So, embrace the good in your life, and hold on to what brings you happiness!

It can be hard to remember all the good when you're trapped in self-pity. But gratitude isn't only about big moments; it's about the little blessings, too. Sometimes, remembering and noticing those little things can make a big difference.

Save Your Energy for Productive Activities

Feeling sorry for yourself takes a lot of your energy, and for what? Making you feel bad? All you're left with when this happens is negativity and exhaustion. So, when you find yourself falling into self-pity, fill your days with productive activities and use your energy for good things instead.

When you act in ways that make it hard to sit around and feel sorry for yourself, you'll have already won half the battle. By not allowing yourself time to ruminate, you are more likely to avoid that feeling altogether. Engage in beloved hobbies, go for a walk, swim, read a book—there are so many options for things you could be doing with your time instead!

Another great activity to engage in when you start wallowing is volunteer work. Not only is this a productive activity, it also involves being compassionate. When you volunteer for a cause you care about, you engage in acts of kindness that matter to you. This motivates you to spend your energy this way and brings you more happiness.

Helping others helps you focus not on what other people should be doing for you, but on all the things you can do for others. It reminds you of all you have to offer the world, which directly fights feelings of worthlessness. It's empowering, helping others, and it's an excellent use of your time and energy.

Self-pity is a way to deconstruct the pain and trauma you have experienced in life. It can, in small doses, help you cope. After all, sometimes taking the time to allow yourself to feel bad is healthy. It's okay to feel low or depressed sometimes. It just shouldn't be a habit.

Try to focus on what's good in your life. For the things that aren't good, work on improving your situation. When it comes down to it, self-pity is a state of mind. It's a pattern of thinking you fall into that shapes your outlook. However, the good news is that it's something you are more than capable of banishing. With only a few simple tricks and changes, you can, once again, feel good about yourself, and be aware of your worth.

Chapter 7

The Choice

Putting an end to your pain

"It takes courage to grow up and become who
you really are."
—E.E. *Cummings*

B y now, you know the power of your thoughts and
you understand that you can think your way into
feeling good and living happily. You know to fine-tune
your thoughts and redirect your focus toward constructive
things. Yet the difficulty, sometimes, lies not in knowing
what to do, but in knowing where to begin. You have all the
tools, but how can you begin to assemble this happy life
without a plan?

Over the years, I've found several ways to fill in the blanks
and learn how to get started on living my fullest life. From
finding your favorite pastimes to creating brand new ones,
I'll show you all kinds of ways to fix the gaps in your life so
you can live better. That is, not just without pain—but with
joy, happiness, and fulfillment.

It All Starts With a Positive Mindset

Many people talk about staying positive and how having the right attitude can make all the difference, but I have a question for you: How many times have you ever listened to someone who gives you practical tips for nurturing a positive attitude?

I don't ask this to put you on the spot, especially since I never listened to that sort of advice when I was still struggling with my past pain. When you're in a dark place, it's hard to listen to people who act like all you need to do to feel happy is to smile more. Honestly, many of the motivational videos out there are kind of bogus. You're a human being, not some software that you can update and reprogram with only a few keystrokes.

Not only that, but there's also an emerging awareness of the harmful effects of toxic positivity. When you're positive to the point that you dismiss any negativity you're experiencing, you aren't fostering a positive attitude. Instead, you're digging yourself deeper into your pain.

Here are some of the traits that contribute to having a positive outlook on life:

Optimism

Many people think optimism and naivety go hand in hand. It seems like an optimistic person is all sunshine and rainbows, all the time! However, that couldn't be further from the truth. Optimism isn't about constantly smiling; it's about living with hope. It's about looking toward the future and seeing happiness.

Optimism is both an attitude and a set of behaviors. It isn't enough to simply hope for the best outcome—you have to put in the work to make that future come to fruition! Optimism is an integral part of what it means to be resilient. After all, how could we be resilient, and constantly forging ahead no matter what life throws our way, if we didn't believe there was something better waiting for us just around the bend?

Optimistic people are more likely to take chances. Where cynics hold themselves back, convinced of their predestined failure, optimists are willing to take that leap of faith. This is because they have faith in themselves, their abilities, and in future possibilities.

There's also a misconception that your personality determines whether or not you're an optimistic person. We think we're either born a happy-go-lucky optimist or a down-to-earth and realistic cynic. The reality is that optimism, just like everything else in life, is a choice. You must actively choose optimism, over and over, even in the face of adversity and hardship.

You don't have to be happy all the time to be an optimist, either. Many people go through periods of anxiety or depression and still are optimists. Sometimes, when life gets hard, and you find yourself facing a crisis—even when everything else seems to fail—optimism is the only thing that will continue to carry you. As I said, the root of optimism lies in both faith and hope—faith in yourself and hope for a promising future.

Acceptance

I've talked about acceptance before. It's a powerful thing, but it can be challenging to learn, and it's an essential part of developing a positive mindset. Acceptance takes strength and courage. It requires you to stop resisting, though, and that's a frightening thought.

Resisting pain is a form of anesthesia. We leave it suspended, perceiving it as an inescapable consequence without end; so we try to live with it. We hide our pain, putting on a mask that transfigures what we perceive, as if feeling pain was a form of weakness. But accepting that pain exists—that it is real, and that it is hurting us— is not weakness at all. On the contrary, it is the strongest thing we can do.

For many people, the moment of acceptance is a turning point. We set ourselves free when we accept the terrible things that have happened and the bad things that may still occur. Acceptance doesn't mean giving in and just letting bad things happen. It's about facing the reality of the situation and acknowledging the truth.

Accepting minor nuisances and inconveniences affects your mood, even beyond the larger struggles. If you're in the car, for example, and seem to be hitting every red light, there's nothing you can do to change that. It's entirely out of your control. Rather than letting resentment and frustration build up as you keep reaching a red, try accepting what's going on and the reality that it is out of your hands.

Once you've accepted the situation, you can let go of your frustration. Instead of using your mental energy to resent what's going on, you can use it for other things. Maybe you can focus on listening to music you enjoy during the drive, or you can admire the scenery around you at each red light; a sight you wouldn't have been able to take in had you hit a green one.

Resilience

Resilience is the ability to recover; to get knocked down and then get back up. It doesn't mean bouncing back immediately, letting hardships slide off us. It doesn't mean you aren't affected by mental struggles, emotional upheavals, or any sort of pain. If you were never affected by these hardships, you wouldn't be resilient.

Being resilient is about learning how to cope with what happens to you. It means carrying on, despite the pain, and eventually reaching a place where you are free. To be resilient means working through your pain so you can come out on the other side. In reading this book, you're demonstrating both your inherent resilience, as well as your commitment to continuing to live with strength.

The Factors of Resilience

Many factors affect how resilient a person might be. Like everything else, resilience is a personal experience that can vary from person to person. Your resilience will not necessarily be built on the same support as someone else. After all, people respond to trauma in different ways, so why wouldn't we recover from trauma differently?

There are, however, a few common support structures that can shape a person's resilience. These factors include things like your support system, self-esteem, communication skills, coping strategies, and emotional regulation, to name a few.

Looking at the different factors that shape resilience, it becomes clear that resilience isn't something that hides

LARA SPADETTO

deep within us only to emerge when we need it most, like some sort of superpower. Instead, it's something that we can work on and foster each and every day.

The Seven Cs of Resilience

Professionals have even developed a roadmap to fostering resilience, known as the seven Cs model of resilience. While this model was created for youths and adolescents as a way to help them prepare for life's challenges, it's something that everyone, no matter what age, can apply to their lives and situations. I'll go through these seven Cs of resilience so you can see how you can apply them to your life.

Competence

When you understand and build upon your strengths, you foster your competence. Competence is your ability to handle things effectively. When you recognize your capabilities and foster your belief in your competence, you set yourself up for understanding your ability to make it through challenging times.

Confidence

Self-confidence is essential. It's intrinsically tied to competence, as without building up your self-esteem, you might never be able to believe in your competency. When you foster your self-confidence, you gain the ability to believe in yourself, which is critical for resilience and having an overall positive outlook.

Connection

We need connection in our lives. When we have strong ties to the people in our lives, we create a support system that we can fall back on in times of hardship. Knowing that there are people who will catch you when you fall makes it easier to get through life's difficulties.

Character

Understanding who you are, what matters to you, and what kind of world you would like to live in are essential parts of resilience. After all, what would be the point of fighting through something if there was nothing worth fighting for?

More than that, understanding when something is wrong helps you learn when you need to be resilient in the first place. So often, when we've experienced trauma, we can grow numb to pain. We accept ill-treatment because it is something to which we have grown accustomed.

When we understand ourselves, we begin to know when we are being mistreated. We recognize when we are trapped in dire situations and when we need to find a way to get out.

Contribution

In this sense, contribution refers to having a sense of purpose. By having goals we are working towards, our gazes turn ahead. Having a forward-facing perspective on life means you are more likely to work through difficulties.

Coping

Healthy coping strategies will always set you up for success. Learning how to manage and deal with stress can be especially helpful when building your resilience. Having healthy outlets for negativity will significantly help you in the face of adversity.

Control

Finally, there's control. I've mentioned before the importance of understanding and accepting that you sometimes can't control life. However, you must never forget the things in life that you can control. That is, your choices. Knowing that you have control over yourself, your decisions, and, often, the outcomes of your choices, is an empowering thing.

Recognizing your control over your reactions and response to life can help free you from toxic mindsets, like self-pity and a victim mentality. As you shape the outcome of your decisions to reach your desired ends, you see all that you are capable of and, in turn, begin to grow in confidence.

Integrity

Integrity also plays a part in having a positive outlook on life. It involves understanding your values, beliefs, and purpose in life. When we live with integrity, we live according to a code that brings meaning to our lives and actions.

Consider, as well, the idea of integrity as bringing together—or integrating—all the various parts of yourself. Since integrity involves being true to who you are, that implies that you must be true to all of you, not just a select few parts. If you try to listen only to your characteristics that are pretty or easy or adhere to a strict set of social norms, you are violating your needs.

Living this way only brings harm, never healing. Living with integrity means never locking parts of yourself away. It means accepting who you are as a whole. Living with integrity means listening to yourself, connecting with who you are inside, and respecting, valuing, and loving what you find.

This concept of integrity aligns with many aspects of self-love, particularly in embracing your strengths and weaknesses. When we listen to and value the whole of our being, we can build a life that aligns with our most authentic set of beliefs.

Living with a positive outlook will help you in so many ways. Mentally, it's a powerful way to fight against negativity, self-pity, and trauma. Emotionally, it can help us overcome and heal from our past trauma and pain, and help us learn to cope with our emotions.

Having this sort of mindset can also significantly affect your physical health. Studies have shown that being optimistic improves heart health, lowers blood pressure, regulates blood sugar levels, and can even help you maintain a healthy weight.

Our state of mind and how our brains function both have a powerful effect on our bodies. When we have a healthy mind, it only follows that we then have a healthy body.

Train Your Brain

Your brain is, without a doubt, the powerhouse of your body. It's the control center, with all experiences, sensations, and instructions falling under its purview. As it controls your mental and physical activities, you need to train your brain to think the right way.

With how many thoughts we have each day—some say over 12000—you don't want the negative to outweigh the positive. According to some speculation, it's believed that a whopping 80 percent of our 12000 daily thoughts are negative.

With this overwhelming and unwanted thought disparity, we must take the time to train our brains to shift away from the negative and towards the positive. With thought awareness boosting your awareness of unhealthy thinking patterns, you're more than ready to start training your brain. I've put together some strategies that I found have helped me create a more positive brain.

Start From the Subconscious

Building from thought awareness, reshaping the thought patterns in your subconscious mind is a powerful way to train your brain. Taking advantage of neuroplasticity to change your brain into a healthy, positive place is a way of shaping your thoughts from the ground up. It creates a solid foundation that you can build upon, as you continue this journey towards positivity.

Neuro-Linguistic Programming

There are many ways you can start to change your brain at the subconscious level. I've mentioned using affirmations and mantras before, and this method falls under the umbrella of neuro-linguistic programming, or NLP.

NLP builds from the understanding that the words and language we use can influence and determine our reality. When we use negative language, we create a negative reality. When we use positive language, we create a positive reality.

This method operates under the belief that every person has a unique map of reality. We may look at the map we have constructed and assume it is a perfect representation of reality—however, that is not the case. Our maps are not, in fact, reality. This means that, as we examine our preconceived notions and biases, we can see how our ways of thinking are wrong. Once that happens, we can redraw the map, making it a more accurate representation of reality.

Think of it this way: You tell yourself you're a failure, so your brain starts to believe that this is true. You begin to see yourself as a failure, over and over, until it becomes a part of you. By using NLP, you examine this belief. Where did it come from, why do you think this way, and how is this holding me back? These are all questions you might ask when confronting the perceived notion.

The more you question, the more you will find that the belief falls apart. You tell yourself that failures are opportunities or that you can overcome your mistakes, and your brain rewires its thought patterns to suit this new reality you are presenting. This is how you create a new map.

Meditation

Meditation is another way you can train your brain. Beyond all of its many impressive benefits—lower stress levels, lower blood pressure, and better sleep, to name a few—meditation also has a powerful effect on the way your brain functions.

Research has shown that meditation can change the structure of your brain, with other research demonstrating how meditation improves your brain's overall function. One of these ways is meditation's ability to improve your focus and reduce your distractibility.

The more focused you are, the less likely you will fall victim to negativity spirals. Negative thoughts won't lead you astray when you have the mental clarity to keep moving towards your goals and stick to your purpose.

When memories of past pain resurface, or you are confronted by emotional triggers, the focus born from meditation will carry you past those events. Rather than chasing unhealthy thoughts down the rabbit hole, you will keep a clear head and persevere.

Letting go of distractions and focusing on the present is the core of mindfulness. Once again, it's clear how intertwined mindfulness and meditation are.

Self-Hypnosis

There are many similarities between meditation and hypnosis, but these two practices are different. While meditation can help you learn to focus on the here and now, hypnosis works best when you enter into a deep state of relaxation. You will be unaware of the world around you in this state, focusing instead on the world within you.

I know it might sound a little out there, but the state of hypnosis is more common than you might think. Have you ever zoned out while doing something, only to regain your focus later and feel somewhat surprised at having finished your task? That's the state hypnosis wants you to achieve.

In this state of relaxation, you will be more suggestible. If you're working with a hypnotherapist, they will guide you through the hypnosis session and provide you with phrases you can employ to rewire your brain. On the other hand, self-hypnosis means you must focus on those phrases yourself.

Combining self-hypnosis with other methods to gain a positive perspective can be a potent tool.

Tapping Techniques

The EFT tapping technique is another way you can improve your mental state. Since this technique, and other techniques like it, focus on recognizing your pain and lowering your stress and anxiety, you learn to recognize and subdue this type of negativity.

These are only some of the ways you can start to reshape your subconscious thought patterns. Experiment with them and see which ones work best for you and your needs.

Create a Positivity Feedback Loop

Like the kindness feedback loop, the positivity feedback loop is when we put positivity into the world and receive positivity in return. This follows the basic premise of the law of attraction: That like attracts like. What we put into the universe is what the universe will provide for us.

When we create this positivity feedback loop, we attract positive people, outcomes, and emotions. When we focus on the positive, we are more likely to see the good things that are in our lives and the good things that have yet to come our way.

Gratitude and optimism are crucial elements of creating a positivity feedback loop. Both of these practices are centered around the idea that it is imperative we consistently remind ourselves of our blessings. We seek out the good, and, in doing so, we can bring even further happiness into our lives.

Focus on What Brings You Happiness

A great way to train your brain to adopt a positive mindset is to redirect your focus on the things that bring you joy. Think of what makes you happy to be alive, and turn your thoughts in that direction.

This can be anything. For some people, it's their friends. For others, it's the way the sunlight hits the surface of a lake. Whatever it is that brings you peace, hold it in the forefront of your thoughts. The more you think about these things, the happier you will be.

One great way to keep track of these things is by journaling. Each day, write down what brought you joy. Try to include various aspects of your life when you do this, such as what makes you happy in your home life and in your career. By having a wide range and covering all the different parts of your life, you'll be able to find joy wherever you are.

Set Aside Time for the Things You Love

Don't just think about the things you love, though! Remember to take time to actually engage with these things, too. The things we are passionate about are often the same things that create meaning in our lives.

I've known many people who stopped taking time to follow their passions for one reason or another. They grew despondent and adrift, and it wasn't until they began to engage with what they loved once more, that the light returned to their lives.

A life without passion is a life without purpose. We weren't meant to exist in this world for the sole purpose of surviving. We were meant to enjoy ourselves, experience beautiful things, and discover the wonders of the world. We were meant to know peace. If your life isn't bringing you bliss, then you should rethink what it is that you're doing.

Making time for your passions can be as simple as setting aside a few minutes each day. We only have so much time in this world; shouldn't we spend it doing what we love?

The Three Daily Positives

The "three good things" is an exercise that is often used in gratitude journaling. While I would recommend trying that exercise out, I've adapted it somewhat so it can work for everyone, even those who might not enjoy journaling.

I like to call this adapted version the "three daily positives." This exercise is an act of reflection. At the end of your day, before you go to sleep for the night, think about three good things that happened that day. These three things can be big or small, since anything positive counts.

Once you have come up with three good things, write them down. After writing them in your journal, reflect on each of them. Think about the reason behind these good things, like what brought them into your life or how they happened. Reflect, as well, on why they brought you happiness.

I love this exercise, as it helps develop an awareness of how the good things in our life come into being and why certain things bring us happiness compared to others. In my adapted version, I suggest taking at least one minute, three times a day, to look around yourself and search for anything positive. Reflect on these positive things the same way you would reflect on your three good things.

What I really like about this exercise is that it combines positive thinking, gratitude, and mindfulness. In short, it emphasizes existence in the present moment. It's a good reminder that positive things exist around us at all times and in any place; we just have to remember to see them.

—————••◦••—————

Finding What You Love

Finding your passion doesn't mean finding a way to do what you love and pay your bills. It also doesn't mean struggling to make a career out of what you love and growing to associate that passion with stress, anxiety, and financial insecurity.

No, finding what you love has a much more significant meaning than that. It's directly related to your life's happiness. Finding what you love and finding your life's happiness is, in many ways, the same thing.

It can be hard to know what you love. Discovering your passion takes trial and error, and what brings joy to the lives of your friends might not bring joy to your life. I've spoken of this before, about finding new and healthy hobbies you can engage in, and how tricky it can be to see the right activity for you.

Often, we think of passion as being something that exists on a large scale. It doesn't have to be, though. Maybe for some people, their passion is earning a million bucks each day, but someone else's passion might be getting a hug from someone they love.

Whatever is the case for you, I've put together a few ways you can find what you love in your life to bring you happiness, joy, and positivity.

Try Many Things

If you don't know where to start, then start anywhere. Finding what you love is an exercise in trial and error and might, unfortunately, be filled with more misses than hits. I mentioned before how much I dislike many forms of exercise. But the only reason I discovered that disliking was because I tried to incorporate these routines into my life during this healing journey.

However, the good news in all this is that you might wind up with a lot of hobbies. While having many hobbies might seem overwhelming, it can be a really good thing. You might even surprise yourself! Sometimes the most unexpected things can wind up being what you enjoy the most.

Introspection

A little introspection never hurts. In fact, it does the opposite. You knock loose a few memories by connecting with your inner self and listening to your needs. Have you ever wanted to try something, but never had the chance? There might be a reason you were drawn to that activity. Often, if you find yourself going back to something over and over, it's because you found it compelling; something about it speaks to you. So, why not listen?

Introspection can also help us remember if we have already found what we love. As you know, one of the effects of depression is an increasing lack of interest in the things you love and enjoy doing. As you recover from your pain, look back on the things you stopped doing and ask yourself if it was because you wanted to, or if it was due to your mental state at the time.

Stay True to Yourself

While I encourage trying new things and even pushing the limits of your comfort zone, if there's something that crosses your boundaries, you should respect that. Listen to your needs, and don't do something that makes you uncomfortable or brings you stress.

An easy example of this is skydiving. While many people have been afraid to go skydiving and then wound up loving it once they did so, these people were probably the types to enjoy thrills in the first place. Some people will simply never want to go skydiving, and that's totally okay!

Remember that staying true to yourself means staying open to changing your mind. It's okay to go through phases. If you liked something at one point but find that it no longer brings you joy, it doesn't make you a failure to stop doing that activity.

We're constantly changing—that's the nature of being human! If it's acceptable for our food or clothing preferences to change over the years, why can't we also change our passions? It doesn't make you fickle or indecisive; it just makes you human.

Let Go of Fear

When I say it's good to push the limits of our comfort zones, this is what I mean. So often, fear holds us back. It keeps us confined in a small, limited space. We tell ourselves that we're happy in this space and convince ourselves that we don't want things that are outside of this zone.

But that's just our fear talking! Test your comfort zone, and see where your fear has overtaken your sense of self. Don't let yourself miss out on good things because you were too afraid to take a chance.

Focus on choosing optimism rather than fear. Choose to believe in a good outcome and take that leap of faith. If you never do this, then you'll never find what you truly love in life. When you're trapped in your fear, you might feel paralyzed, but just remember that all you have to do is take those few steps and open the door. Once you're outside, you'll remember all the possibilities stretching out before you.

Make Decisions

To find your passions, you have to be willing to make choices. Sometimes those choices won't pan out, but you can't let the fear of that happening stop you. When you find yourself worrying over a possible negative outcome of your decision, think instead of the good that might come from it.

Choose, as well, to put yourself first. Decide to prioritize your wants and needs as you go through this journey of self-discovery. When you choose to focus on yourself rather than someone else, you'll be free.

Don't Worry About Universal Acceptance

There isn't a single person in this world who is universally beloved. Even great humanitarians have their critics. If you spend your life trying to please everyone, you'll never find happiness. How could you expect to find your passion if you're catering to the passions of others?

Don't waste time explaining your goals, dreams, and passions to people you know will never understand them. If someone is open to listening and learning, then, by all means, explain away!

Live the life you want to live and try to be the person you want to be. Take care and listen to yourself. Nobody can live your life in your place; others can only offer you their opinions. The one who has to carry out the actions is you.

Whether you're receiving honor or blame, try to always have a compass in hand. Sometimes you find yourself in the middle of a sandstorm and you lose direction, but accepting responsibility for your actions and knowing where you want to go is essential to continue your journey.

Keeping this in mind, try not to hurt others, as the pain caused to another person is pain done to ourselves. It becomes an even deeper wound because it is sealed by shame and the awareness of what we have done.

Surround yourself with positive people, with whom you share values ⊓⊓and projects, and who push you to be a better version of yourself.

Hobbies for Healing

Why not try testing out some healing hobbies as you search for your passion? It's always a good idea to indulge in activities that draw your attention away from the traumas and inhibitions of your past pain.

When you do this, not only do you have the opportunity to engage in interesting and fun activities, but you also gain the strength to break free from the pain that keeps you shackled to your past.

In the truest sense, participating in healing hobbies—that is, hobbies that are proven to be beneficial to your mental health—is an act of self-care. So, why not take some time for yourself and try out some of these wonderful and healing hobbies? Who knows, maybe one of these will wind up being your passion!

Painting

Painting is the passion that has sustained me in many moments of my life.

It has always been present, even if in some periods I have neglected it. Painting is the love to which I have always returned. Like a faithful friend, it is always with me in both happy and dark times. The introspection induced by the brush on the surface helps me to channel emotions, feelings, and thoughts.

While I paint, I enter a trance where time has no meaning anymore. My focus is totally on the present moment, and reality enters a parallel dimension. It is like meditating; the thoughts disappear and only the canvas and the colors remain.

There have even been studies done that show how beneficial painting is to mental health. It reduces stress levels, creates positive feelings, and can help induce a sense of mindfulness as you focus on the canvas in front of you. Whether you've painted before or not, I highly recommend giving this hobby a try.

Gardening

Gardening is a great way to de-stress. From growing your own vegetables to cultivating beautiful flowers, gardening offers so many opportunities for you to find a new and fun hobby. Gardening isn't only for people who have enough space to do so, either. With more and more people turning to indoor gardening, even apartment-dwellers can engage in this hobby.

Gardening has been proven to have a beneficial effect on your mental health. There's even a type of therapy known as horticultural therapy. This therapy can help people struggling with trauma, grief, depression, and many other mental struggles.

Music

Music has long been known to be incredibly healing. Just think of the commonality of music therapy; it can tap into your emotions and make you connect with and feel things on an intense and genuine level. Listening to music, singing, and playing an instrument are great ways to engage in this healing hobby.

Music can be calming, invigorating, inspiring, and even help you focus. No matter what it is that you need, music can likely provide it.

Arts and Crafts

Engaging in arts and crafts is another incredibly healing hobby. This includes all sorts of activities, like coloring, knitting, crocheting, drawing, origami, and so much more. These hobbies are a great way to express your emotions and tap into your creative energy. They're also known to help reduce stress and anxiety.

These sorts of creative activities also provide you with a sense of completion and the satisfaction that so often accompanies it. This is because when you finish your painting, knitting project, or whatever activity it was, you have a tangible piece of evidence that you did something. It's a powerful thing to hold, in your own hands, something you have made physically.

Creative Writing

Much like arts and crafts, creative writing is an excellent way to tap into your creative side and express your emotions. Short stories, poems, or even full-length novels are all wonderful ways to engage with creative writing.

This hobby really can become a passion project. When you write something—not for anyone else, simply for yourself—you might feel utterly free, simply because you want to. It's a beautiful way to put a piece of yourself into the world; to express yourself in ways you might not have been able to before.

Cooking

The act of cooking can improve your mental health, and the delicious food you get to eat after doesn't hurt either! Cooking is a beautiful act of love, whether cooking for someone else or for yourself. Taking the time to make a meal can boost your mood and confidence when you get to taste and enjoy the results of all your hard work and effort.

Hiking

Hiking through nature can bring you an immense sense of peace. Not only is it a healthy and physical activity, meaning it's good for your body, but it also gives you a chance to reconnect with nature. We should take time away from technology once in a while and surround ourselves with the healing power of the natural world.

Even as short a walk as five minutes can benefit your mood. The longer you hike, though, the more benefits you'll experience. It doesn't have to be a strenuous or challenging hike, either. An easy hike has as much of a mental benefit as any other kind.

Photography

Whether you know what you're doing or not, photography is a fun and engaging hobby. It's calming, sometimes, to pick a place and wait for the perfect moment to take a picture. In many ways, photography reinforces mindfulness, as you must focus on the present world to get the perfect shot.

Photography also teaches us to appreciate the beauty that exists around us. Even the most mundane things can be transformed into something stunning through a camera lens. The more we begin to see the beauty in the everyday world around us through our camera, the more we'll start to see that same beauty through our own eyes.

Learning a New Language

Learning a new language is an enriching experience! Not only that, but it's a lot of fun. When you learn a new language, you might envision a future where you travel to a place that speaks this language and navigate it without too much trouble.

You might even want to learn the language to read a book in its original tongue. Whatever your reason, learning a new language is a fun and productive use of your time. It doesn't matter if you become an expert, either—just the act of learning is something that can bring immense joy.

Healing hobbies like learning a new language, painting, writing, music, hiking, and the many others I have discussed are all activities that will bring you joy. Try these different activities and experience their many benefits for yourself, as you work towards peace.

Happiness is not a permanent state. It doesn't last forever like in fairy tales, but instead it is in continuous, fluctuating movement.

It is inevitable to be constantly looking for what makes us happy. Even when it seems that we have achieved it, after a while, the feeling of joy goes out and we have to start the search over again.

For this reason, we must learn to use positive tools that help us on this journey.

The path must be chosen with awareness to ensure that the survival autopilot does not take us in a direction that seems easier, but is actually more difficult.

Chapter 8

Rebirth

Hitting the reset button

"Every new beginning comes from some other
beginning's end."
—*Seneca*

E ven now, you might feel gripped with fear and anxiety when you think about your life. It's common to lose focus and become distracted, especially when you've just escaped a storm. After all, when you're in the middle of the downpour, it can be hard to remember how it feels to have the sunshine warm your skin. Even when it stops raining, you're still drenched. When you're shivering, it's easy to miss the warmth shining down on you.

This is why you must try to remember this simple truth: There is always a tomorrow. The rain will end, the sun will rise, and a new day will always follow in the wake of an old one. No matter what happens, no matter what hardships and obstacles and pain present themselves, there is always hope, ready to carry us through. This hope is what we must cling to, as it is the hope to start anew.

Rebooting Your Life Mojo

Starting anew is a scary thing! It's especially so when you're feeling emotionally delicate. Failed relationships, raising kids, growing responsibilities—these are all ingredients in the cocktail of life and its many challenges. Sometimes these different tasks can be overwhelming for even the world's strongest people, let alone anyone who has gone through or is currently going through a hard time!

There's the added difficulty, too, of re-learning who you are. Sometimes it can feel like you've become an entirely new person without even realizing it. Where do you even start with that seemingly monumental task? Even if you've learned how to let go of the past, what comes next? How do you move forward?

What you need to remember is that, while it might seem daunting, you absolutely can start over. Starting over is a pretty standard part of life. We're told that life is linear, that we should stay on one course and move from one milestone to the next with perfect progression, but how many people can honestly say they've lived that way?

Starting over and trying new things is part of what makes life interesting. As we evolve, our needs evolve along with us. Remember that starting over isn't failing. It's just a step in a new direction.

There are things to consider when rebooting your life. Financial considerations are one of the biggest reasons people stay trapped in their old lives. It can seem impossible to start over when dealing with financial stresses, such as debt. But you don't have to let money anxiety rule your life. Making a budget, learning about the debt cycle, and generally taking care of your overall stress levels can make financial problems feel more manageable.

Sometimes we're forced to reboot our lives in ways we never expected. Divorce is one of these times. You go into a marriage thinking you made a lifelong commitment, and then, suddenly, it's not that. It's hard going from being someone in a relationship to being single again.

Divorce can leave you lonely, depressed, and grieving. It's important to feel these emotions to kickstart the healing process, but it's also essential to make sure they don't consume you. keep in mind, there is life after divorce! You can restart. So many people have, and they're happier than ever.

Remember that you can always pick yourself back up, no matter what the situation is. When the waters have calmed and the storm has settled, you can move forward to stand beneath the sun. Here are a few ways you can begin to rebuild your life after the proverbial storm:

Reboot Your Inner Self

Life looks different after going through hardships, and there's a chance you're probably different, too! Instead of trying to recreate your life to be the same as before the pain, you should try to get to know the new you. Even without past pain, you would be different from who you were in the past, as people are constantly changing. Don't look at this evolution as a consequence of your suffering. Instead, see it as a natural step in living.

When you reboot your life, you're given an opportunity to reboot your inner self. Check in with yourself and reflect on your inner values, life goals, and needs. If any of these things have shifted in some way, that means it's time to create a plan of action to incorporate these new outlooks into your life as you advance.

If you no longer want to achieve the goals you once did, take the time to consider what you now want from life. Maybe you were more career-oriented before, whereas now you would rather prioritize the time outside of work. Whatever the case, make the most of this turning point in your life.

Questioning yourself can be a tricky thing, and it can be even harder to come to terms with the idea that what you've worked for might no longer be something that brings you joy. You might try to convince yourself that, since you've put in all that work, you might as well keep forging ahead on this path; that maybe one day you'll go back to feeling how you felt before.

That way of thinking does more harm than good and aligns with something known as the sunk-cost fallacy. This fallacy explains people's tendency to follow through with something, even if it is no longer worthwhile or suitable for them. If they have invested something in that endeavor, be it time, money, or effort, it is difficult to walk away from it.

We believe that we should see it through to the end, simply because we worked at something. This keeps us trapped in unhealthy relationships, careers, and other lifestyles that we might be better off leaving behind.

When you've gone through a hard time, you try to cling to the familiar as a way to find comfort. By checking in and rebooting your inner self, you can see all how those old familiar paths are no longer leading you to the right destination.

Understanding what you value helps you create a life that you value. If you aren't living according to what you love, your life will feel unfulfilling. To reflect on who you are, what you want, and what you need—then with time—you'll find yourself living a life with meaning.

Work on Your Love Life

When I say work on your love life, I don't only mean your romantic love life. Familial and platonic bonds are still bonds of love. Remembering to value and cherish these bonds can be crucial in resetting your life.

However, this doesn't mean you shouldn't work on your romantic love life, either! When we've been burned in relationships before, we might find ourselves shying away from the flame. But it's important to remember that not every relationship is going to scorch us. A life filled with love is a life filled with light, and you don't want to lose that light for fear of fire.

Working on your love life also means working on your relationships with yourself. Self-love, after all, is the foundation upon which you can build all other love connections. Treat yourself with kindness, and you will treat others with kindness in turn.

Take a look at the relationships in your life, with others and with yourself. If any of them are toxic, then now is the time to learn how to either repair those relationships or let them go entirely. Look, as well, at the times you have been toxic in a relationship. If you have hurt the people in your life, try to make amends. If the people in your life have hurt you, let them know how you feel in a calm, level-headed way. Relationships are a bridge between people. It takes both sides to anchor this connection in place.

Finding the balance within yourself has priority; there's no need to jump into anything. Go at your own pace, and do what feels right to you. If you aren't ready to start dating, that's fine! If you aren't prepared to welcome back someone who has hurt you, that's fine, as well. Do what feels right for you. What matters is that you're prioritizing your relationship with yourself.

Remember, though, to make sure that you aren't avoiding certain aspects of your love life out of fear. It's one thing to take the time to put yourself first because it's what's best for you; it's another thing entirely to use that as an excuse to hide away.

Get Your Home in Order

Your home should be your safe space. It should be the ultimate source of comfort. Somewhere you feel like you'll always belong. Having a healthy home life plays a huge role in leading a happy life. An out-of-order home can be an enormous source of worry.

When you're going through a hard time, your home life can sometimes fall by the wayside. This is because a lot of us take our home lives for granted. We tell ourselves they'll always be there, and, due to this perspective, we can lose sight of our homes.

Sometimes your home life can be the source of your pain. When that happens, your home becomes hostile. It can make finding and creating another home a more daunting task going forward. The idea of security in the home feels impermanent, and you might find yourself waiting for the other shoe to drop.

This is why I recommend getting your home life in order after going through a hard time, whether your pain is centered in the home or not. A happy and healthy home life typically includes three factors: Familial relationships, the overall atmosphere, and the running of the home.

Familial relationships are essentially the cornerstone of home life. When you have healthy relationships with the others living in your home, your home's energy becomes positive. Reach out to your family members and try to connect with them.

Strengthen and foster your bonds, and try to share meaningful time. Not only will this help your home life, it will help you create new, positive memories that you can use as a focus when you need to remind yourself of the good things in your life.

Your family might also be able to help you come up with a plan for moving forward. Maybe they could have some insights into your needs that you didn't even realize. Sometimes it takes an outside perspective to be able to see things clearly. If you feel you're able, try to lean on your biological and chosen family to help you move forward.

The atmosphere of the home is the same as the home's energy. Have you ever walked into someone's house and found it warm and inviting? Alternatively, have you ever walked into someone's house and found it cold or austere? These are examples of a home's atmosphere. If your home was once fraught and filled with negativity, it's essential to find a way to clear out that destructive energy.

Redecorating can be a way to reset your home's atmosphere. Painting the walls, buying a new rug, or even rearranging the furniture can help you create distance between your home during the difficult times and your home now.

However, sometimes all you need to do to revitalize the atmosphere of your home is live with positivity. It's the law of attraction, after all! As you live in positivity, the space around you will fill with that same light.

Finally, changing how your home runs can significantly affect your mood. There's a lot of anxiety around having the perfect home. Trying to keep up appearances is an immense drain on your energy, and, like perfectionism, it's always going to be a losing battle.

Work together with your partner, your children, or other family members to find a way to live together harmoniously. The way you exist in your home should benefit you; it shouldn't be a performance to impress strangers.

Give Yourself Space

Sometimes we become so caught up in the idea of restarting our lives and heading in a new, positive direction, that we wind up overdoing things. We burn ourselves out and, in doing so, create unnecessary anxiety, stress, and possibly even depression around something that should be positive.

It's important to give yourself time and space when rebooting your life. Give yourself the room you need to figure things out. Let yourself make wrong choices and learn to be okay with that. Plan your next steps, and don't allow yourself to feel guilty if it takes you longer than you thought it would to get started.

When you push yourself too hard, you create resentment, even towards things you love. Healing is a process, and it's not linear in any way, shape, or form. It's a winding path with many trails splitting off in different directions.

Sometimes you need to think before choosing which path to take. Sometimes, even when you take that time, you might still choose the wrong path and need to double back.

All of that is perfectly okay. If you need physical space to heal, find a way to create that distance. If you need some emotional space, explain that to your loved ones and help them figure out ways they can help you, while still respecting your boundaries.

It's okay to take time to figure out what you need. It's also okay to know what you need, but take time before getting started. Sometimes a little space, time, and healing are what make all the difference in your journey.

Seek Professional Help

Sometimes what will help the most is reaching out to a professional. It's a scary idea— opening up to a stranger about your trauma—but it's also incredibly beneficial. This person is trained to help people just like you, people who have gone through suffering and come out the other side.

It also helps to talk to someone who doesn't know you or doesn't have any preconceived notions. Your friends and family might not be able to provide you with the unbiased and non-judgmental perspective that a trained professional can.

If you think professional help is the right choice for you, I encourage you to pursue this course of action. Sometimes we need more help than our loved ones can provide. There is no shame in needing that help. It's a sign of strength to recognize when you need help, after all.

Working for Tomorrow—Tips to Recreate Your Life

While those are all great ways to restart your life once the hardships have passed, you don't have to wait for that time. Perhaps you're in a situation right now where you feel as though all hope is lost. You think you've hit a dead-end, that nothing is ever going to work out, and all that's left for you is to sink into the depths of despair.

If this is your situation, just remember: Hope is never entirely lost. Like the sun at night, it is always there, just waiting for dawn. No matter how dire your life feels, being hopeful and taking some necessary actions can make all the difference in the world.

Remember that there is good on the other side of your pain and that something beautiful is waiting for you. So, when you find yourself in need of a change in your life, you can try some of these tips I've put together as a way to bring about that change.

Reconsider Your Habits

When you're in the middle of a painful situation, you want to focus on smaller, more manageable tasks to help you work for a better tomorrow, rather than the big picture items that accompany rebooting your life.

One of the first things you can do is recognize that the way you have been living is not healthy. People are incredibly adaptable, and we grow used to the environment in which we find ourselves. In terms of physical survival, this is hugely beneficial. If you were used to living somewhere warm, for example, and then moved somewhere cold, your ability to adapt to these new, lower temperatures can help alleviate your discomfort.

However, when it comes to overcoming pain and trauma, this adaptability isn't such a good thing. You can become accustomed to pain, so you go through your life with that pain, forgetting that you can do something to eliminate it.

This is why it's essential to rethink your behavioral patterns. When you feel lost in a hopeless situation, look at how you have been living. Have you been challenging your pain, or have you been accommodating it?

Consider your habits and question why they are habits in the first place. Do you sleep until after ten because you aren't a morning person, or is it because you're delaying getting out of bed? Pay attention to your routines and see what can and should be overhauled for you to make a fresh start.

See if there are things in your life that you feel no longer represent you, but that you don't change, because you are used to them. Does the effort to change them seem greater than that of continuing to live with them as before?

Getting used to what hurts us reminds me of the "myth of the boiled frog." This myth is used as a metaphor to explain how easy it is to adapt to habits that are sometimes harmful. Just like the frog, we grow accustomed to what is happening until it becomes impossible to get out of the situation.

Take your career, for example; are you happy with it? If not, then it might be worth looking into different possible options. If it is, then take a look at things like your workplace environment, your performance, and your relationships with your colleagues. See if there are any areas in your career that you've been putting up with, and see what you can do to change them from something you must endure to something positive.

When you're in the middle of a hard time, it's difficult to see all the little ways you're facilitating those hardships. By dismantling the idea of business, as usual, you open up space for new and exciting change.

Declutter Your Life

Sometimes cleaning house—both figuratively and literally—can be the push you need to start making changes in your life. Go through all your material belongings and see what you no longer need. You might be surprised at what you find you're ready to let go of.

We put a lot of emotional weight on physical items. Maybe someone gave you something, so you hang onto it, not wanting to lose that memory. In many cases, that sentimentality can be a beautiful thing. A grandmother's necklace, for example, is a treasured item that carries many memories.

However, sometimes we hang onto objects and memories that hurt us. If an ex-partner gave you something and now, every time you see it, you're reminded of the end of that relationship, you should probably let that item go. Removing physical reminders of emotional pain not only cuts down on excess possessions in your home, but also helps to clear out the emotional clutter you may have been unknowingly harboring.

Get in Shape for What's Next

To become emotionally ready to fight through your trauma and pain to prepare to reboot your life, sometimes you have to get in shape. Mentally preparing yourself for the hard work to come is one of these steps, as is taking better care of your body. After all, the mind and body are so closely and deeply intertwined. When you take care of one part of yourself, you take care of all the parts of yourself.

Eating healthy, looking into healing hobbies, reading up on healthy coping mechanisms, and incorporating exercise into your life are all ways you can get in shape for what's next in your life.

Pay It Forward

It might seem counterintuitive, but sometimes the best way to pull yourself out of a slump is to help someone else do that exact thing. Acts of kindness bring kindness and happiness into your life, and generosity is proven to boost your mental health and energy.

Take the kindness that others have given you during your struggles and share that same kindness with others who might be in need. Even something as simple as smiling at someone, saying a few kind words, or letting them move ahead of you in line when they're in a rush, can make all the difference.

When we foster a culture of passing on kindness, we find ourselves surrounded by positivity. The compassion you give to someone else will one day make its way back to you. This creates a support system that you can use to help you, and others like you, learn to see hope in the world around you.

Starting fresh often seems more daunting than it is. Instead of letting fear consume you, lock your gaze on the future possibilities, and put in the work towards resetting your life. These hacks I've provided are all ways you can get that work started, no matter where you are in your life. Whether you're in the pit or you've recently climbed out, you can move past your trauma and take these first steps towards creating a brighter future.

Conclusion

L ife is hard. It's painful and challenging, and sometimes it seems like it's out to get you, throwing hardships in your path time and time again. But that isn't all there is to life. Life can be wonderful. It can be kind, generous, and filled with incredible opportunities. The truth is that, while there are certainly events, experiences, and situations that are out of your control, a large part of how your life unfurls is due to what you make of it.

I talked about the burden on your shoulders, and how the pain we've experienced becomes a burden we carry throughout our days. I hope that, by this point, a little bit of that pain has lessened. I hope that your shoulders are a little bit lighter.

Remember, the first steps to letting go of what has hurt you, and learning to heal from your past trauma and pain, are up to you. Learn to challenge your negative thoughts. Reframe your perspective and take note of the world around you. Look at the blessings that already exist in your life, and use those blessings to further your resolve as you move forward.

Ask yourself the same thing my friend asked me: What is right about my situation that I am not getting?

Using the tips, tricks, and life hacks that I've discussed in this book, you have all the tools you need to heal. It's a hard thing, learning to let go of your pain, and some days it might seem entirely impossible, but I can tell you it's worth a try. I've lived through it as well. I know your struggles because I have struggled with those same things, and although I am aware that my journey is a constant and continuous work, I find it extremely fascinating to discover that, while we all have the tools at hand, it is entirely up to us to put them into action.

Remember what you have learned in this book when you find yourself spiraling. Remember that you are not your thoughts and that the negativity born from your trauma does not and should not define you.

Treat yourself with kindness and compassion. This is truly the only way forward. It's hard to grant yourself grace when, for so long, you have only granted yourself suffering. Breaking these old behavioral patterns and building new ones upon a foundation of compassion will be the beginning of a new chapter in your life. This new chapter will mark the part of your story where you control the narrative.

Self-love will lead you to freedom; freedom from negativity, self-criticism, self-doubt, and the toxic pursuit of perfectionism. It will free you from the bonds built by shame and guilt. Self-love is how you can learn to live in this world, free of pain, trauma, and upsetting memories. When you learn to treat yourself with compassion, you will learn to live for yourself.

I think that's something many of us struggle to remember, especially when we have other people to care for in our lives: We forget that our lives should be ours. A large part of the process of overcoming your pain is realizing that you deserve so much more. You deserve to live a life of kindness, light, and love. You deserve to live with meaning, and you deserve to live according to your values.

Set an example to the rest of the world by treating yourself with compassion. Show your friends, your family, and even new acquaintances that you are someone who recognizes their worth. You understand you are a being deserving of respect and consideration, same as everyone else.

Our eyes can adjust to the dark. We can see shapes, make out figures, and we may even be able to navigate through a darkened hallway without bumping into any furniture or door frames. But isn't it so much clearer when you turn on a light?

That's what letting go of your past pain is like. You can live with the pain; you have lived with the pain. But life is so much better once you begin to let yourself heal. I urge you to stop living with your pain, simply because it's something you have grown comfortable with. You deserve better than a life like that. Life can be full of purpose and meaning; you have just to be willing to try.

You can live the life you want and deserve. I believe this with my whole heart. All you have to do is dare to let go of your past and face the future head-on. So go and, using all the tools you found here, reach for that brilliant future!

References

- Ackerman, C. (2021, December 6). *What is self-awareness and why is it important? [+5 ways to increase it].* Positive Psychology. https://positivepsychology.com/self-awareness-matters-how-you-can-be-more-self-aware/
- American Psychological Association. (2011). *Strategies for controlling your anger: Keeping anger in check.* American Psychological Association. https://www.apa.org/topics/anger/strategies-controlling
- American Psychological Association. (2017, July). *What is cognitive behavioral therapy?* American Psychological Association. https://www.apa.org/ptsd-guideline/patients-and-families/cognitive-behavioral
- Andre Maurois Quotes. (n.d.). Brainy Quote. Retrieved March 8, 2022, from BrainyQuote.com: https://www.brainyquote.com/quotes/andre_maurois_158006
- Angelo, J. (2016, February 15). *The importance of home.* Spirituality & Health. https://www.spiritualityhealth.com/articles/2016/02/15/importance-home
- Anonymous. (2012, July 11). *The power of acceptance: Stop resisting and find the lesson.* Tiny Buddha.

https://tinybuddha.com/blog/the-power-of-accepta
nce-stop-resisting-and-find-the-lesson/

• Anthony, K. (2018, September 18). EFT *tapping*.
Healthline.
https://www.healthline.com/health/eft-tapping

• Beasley, E. (2021, March 29). *Best hobbies for mental
health*. Healthgrades.
https://www.healthgrades.com/right-care/mental-he
alth-and-behavior/best-hobbies-for-mental-health

• Beresin, E. (2014, February 16). *The power of resilience*.
Psychology Today.
https://www.psychologytoday.com/ca/blog/inside-o
ut-outside-in/201402/the-power-resilience-0

• Boduryan-Turner, M. (2021, February 16). *Self-Love:
The most important love of your life*. Embracing You
Therapy.
https://embracingyoutherapy.com/self-love-the-most
-important-love-of-your-life/

• Bondarenko, P. (2015, November 23). *Sunk cost*.
Encyclopedia Britannica.
https://www.britannica.com/topic/sunk-cost

• Borges, A. (2020a, September 1). *How to meditate
when you have no idea where to start*. SELF.
https://www.self.com/story/how-to-meditate

• Borges, A. (2020b, September 23). *Do yourself a favor
and write down your negative thoughts*. SELF.
https://www.self.com/story/write-down-negative-th
oughts

• Brantley Agency. (2017, October 18). *How to train your
brain to go positive instead of negative*. Brantley Agency.
https://www.brantleyagency.com/train-brain-go-posi
tive-instead-negative/

• Brennan, D. (2021, October 25). *What to know about
emotional health*. WebMD.

https://www.webmd.com/balance/what-to-know-about-emotional-health

• Brenner, G. (2014, August 4). *The beauty and ease of accepting things as they are.* Dr. Gail Brenner. https://gailbrenner.com/2014/08/the-beauty-and-ease-of-accepting-things-as-they-are/

• Brody, J. E. (2017, March 27). *A positive outlook may be good for your health.* The New York Times. https://www.nytimes.com/2017/03/27/well/live/positive-thinking-may-improve-health-and-extend-life.html

• Brzosko, M. (2017, December 12). *Overcome negative thinking: Take charge of your thoughts.* Better Humans. https://betterhumans.pub/want-to-be-happier-how-to-take-charge-of-your-thoughts-e74ad496aced

• Burton, N. (2016, January 7). *What are basic emotions?* Psychology Today. https://www.psychologytoday.com/intl/blog/hide-and-seek/201601/what-are-basic-emotions

• Cafasso, J. (2021, April 12). *Traumatic events.* Healthline. https://www.healthline.com/health/traumatic-events

• Campbell, P. (2020, February 20). *The power of optimistic action.* Psychology Today. https://www.psychologytoday.com/us/blog/imperfect-spirituality/202002/the-power-optimistic-action

• Cherry, K. (2021, April 5). *The 6 types of basic emotions and their effect on human behavior.* Verywell Mind. https://www.verywellmind.com/an-overview-of-the-types-of-emotions-4163976

• Chopra, D. (2013). What are you hungry for? : The Chopra solution to permanent weight loss, well-being, and lightness of soul. Harmony.

• Chui, A. (2013, October 10). *12 simple ways you can build a positive attitude.* Lifehack.

https://www.lifehack.org/articles/communication/12-simple-ways-you-can-build-positive-attitude.html

• Dixon, A. (2011, September 6). *Kindness makes you happy...and happiness makes you kind.* Greater Good. https://greatergood.berkeley.edu/article/item/kindness_makes_you_happy_and_happiness_makes_you_kind

• Drew Gerald Quotes. (n.d.) What Should I Read Next. Retrieved March 8, 2022, from WhatShouldIReadNext.com: https://www.whatshouldireadnext.com/quotes/drew-gerald-look-outside-and-you-will

• Dworkin-McDaniel, N. (2017, November 15). *Life after divorce: 12 ways to rebuild your life.* Everyday Health. https://www.everydayhealth.com/emotional-health/life-after-divorce-12-ways-rebuild-your-life/

• Eckhart Tolle Quotes (n.d.) Good Reads. Retrieved March 8, 2022, from GoodReads.com: https://www.goodreads.com/quotes/47872-you-find-peace-not-by-rearranging-the-circumstances-of-your

• E. E. Cummings Quotes. (n.d.). Brainy Quote. Retrieved March 8, 2022, from BrainyQuote.com: https://www.brainyquote.com/quotes/e_e_cummings_161593

• Fahkry, T. (2017, October 27). *If you want to be happy, accept life as it is and let go of what you cannot control.* Medium; Mission.org. https://medium.com/the-mission/if-you-want-to-be-happy-accept-life-as-it-is-and-let-go-of-what-you-cannot-control-466ac638a45b

• Ferrari, M., Yap, K., Scott, N., Einstein, D. A., & Ciarrochi, J. (2018). Self-compassion moderates the perfectionism and depression link in both adolescence and adulthood. PLOS ONE, 13(2), e0192022. https://doi.org/10.1371/journal.pone.0192022

* George Bernard Shaw Quotes. (n.d.) Good Reads. Retrieved March 8, 2022, from GoodReads.com: https://www.goodreads.com/quotes/194072-you-don -t-stop-laughing-when-you-grow-old-you-grow
* George Orwell Quotes. (n.d.). Brainy Quotes. Retrieved March 8, 2022, from BrainyQuote.com: https://www.brainyquote.com/quotes/george_orwell _119587
* Gillette, H. (2021, September 7). *How to recognize and redirect self-pity.* Psych Central. https://psychcentral.com/blog/self-pity-to-self-com passion?c=917089152543
* Gouin, J.-P., Kiecolt-Glaser, J. K., Malarkey, W. B., & Glaser, R. (2008). The influence of anger expression on wound healing. *Brain, Behavior, and Immunity, 22*(5), 699–708. https://doi.org/10.1016/j.bbi.2007.10.013
* Hafner, D. (2014, November 5). *When you start to let go of your past, these 10 things will happen.* Lifehack. https://www.lifehack.org/articles/communication/w hen-you-start-let-your-past-these-10-things-will-hap pen.html
* Healthwise Staff. (2020, August 31). *Tapping the power of optimism.* University of Michigan Health System; Healthwise. https://www.uofmhealth.org/health-library/abl0330
* Ho, L. (2021, June 4). *How to start over and reboot your life when it seems too late.* Lifehack. https://www.lifehack.org/810843/how-to-start-over
* Hurley, K. (2020, December 11). *What is resilience? Your guide to facing life's challenges, adversities, and crises.* EverydayHealth. https://www.everydayhealth.com/wellness/resilience /

- Hurst, K. (2017a, January 10). *6 ways to train your subconscious mind for positive thinking*. The Law of Attraction. https://www.thelawofattraction.com/6-ways-train-brain-stay-positive/
- Hurst, K. (2017b, November 2). *Self hypnosis for success: How to achieve your goals in life*. The Law of Attraction. https://www.thelawofattraction.com/self-hypnosis-achieve-goals/
- John F. Kennedy Quotes. (n.d.). Brainy Quote. Retrieved March 8, 2022, from BrainyQuote.com: https://www.brainyquote.com/quotes/john_f_kennedy_121068
- Johnstone, D. (2014, July 11). *8 ways to let go of self-pity for good*. Lifehack. https://www.lifehack.org/articles/communication/why-and-how-let-your-self-pity.html
- Kelly, A. (2019, May 29). *Are you self-critical?* Psychology Today. https://www.psychologytoday.com/us/blog/all-about-attitude/201905/are-you-self-critical
- Kero, A. (2021, August 4). *10 ways to reinvent yourself when you're stuck in life*. Everyday Power. https://everydaypower.com/reinvent-yourself/
- Khoshaba, D. (2012, March 27). *A seven-step prescription for self-love*. Psychology Today. https://www.psychologytoday.com/us/blog/get-hardy/201203/seven-step-prescription-self-love
- Kiken, L. G., & Shook, N. J. (2014). Does mindfulness attenuate thoughts emphasizing negativity, but not positivity? *Journal of Research in Personality, 53*, 22–30. https://doi.org/10.1016/j.jrp.2014.08.002
- Kim, E. S., Hagan, K. A., Grodstein, F., DeMeo, D. L., De Vivo, I., & Kubzansky, L. D. (2016). Optimism and

cause-specific mortality: A prospective cohort study. *American Journal of Epidemiology*, 185(1), 21–29. https://doi.org/10.1093/aje/kww182

- Krishna. (2019, September 30). *What does it mean to be A positive thinker?* Superprof. https://www.superprof.co.in/blog/what-are-positive -thinking-skills/

- Kubzansky, L. D., Sparrow, D., Vokonas, P., & Kawachi, I. (2001). Is the glass half empty or half full? A prospective study of optimism and coronary heart disease in the normative aging study. *Psychosomatic Medicine*, 63(6), 910–916. https://doi.org/10.1097/00006842-200111000-00009

- Lawrence, E. M., Rogers, R. G., & Wadsworth, T. (2015). Happiness and longevity in the United States. *Social Science & Medicine*, 145, 115–119. https://doi.org/10.1016/j.socscimed.2015.09.020

- Leonard, J. (2021, March 4). *How to let go of the past: Tips for relationships, regret, and trauma.* Medical News Today. https://www.medicalnewstoday.com/articles/how-to -let-go-of-the-past

- Lian, M. (n.d.). *How to start over in life when you feel stuck.* Thrive Global. https://thriveglobal.com/stories/how-to-start-over-i n-life-when-you-feel-stuck/

- Lindberg, S. (2018, August 31). *How to let go of things from the past.* Healthline. https://www.healthline.com/health/how-to-let-go

- Loggins, B. (2021, November 23). *Signs of childhood trauma in adults.* Verywell Mind. https://www.verywellmind.com/signs-of-childhood-t rauma-in-adults-5207979

- Lucid Content Team. (2018, February 6). *The ultimate goal setting process: 7 steps to creating better goals.* Lucid

Chart.
https://www.lucidchart.com/blog/the-ultimate-goal-setting-process-in-7-steps

• Mager, D. (2017, January 17). *8 strategies to work through anger and resentment*. Psychology Today.
https://www.psychologytoday.com/gb/blog/some-assembly-required/201701/8-strategies-work-through-anger-and-resentment

• Marshall, C. (2021, February 12). *How to (really) practice self love: 4 things to remember*. Self Space.
https://theselfspace.com/how-to-really-practice-self-love-4-things-to-remember/

• McCabe, C. (2021, February 15). *The science behind why hobbies can improve our mental health*. Connecting Research; University of Reading.
https://research.reading.ac.uk/research-blog/the-science-behind-why-hobbies-can-improve-our-mental-health/

• Mead, E. (2022, April 2). *What are negative emotions and how to control them?* Positive Psychology.
https://positivepsychology.com/negative-emotions/

• Mental Health Center. (2019, April 3). *How childhood trauma affects us as adults*. Mental Health Center.
https://www.mentalhealthcenter.org/how-childhood-trauma-affects-adult-relationships/

• Migala, J. (2021, June 28). *How to start over when life's got you down: 7 steps to launching a comeback*. Women's Health.
https://www.womenshealthmag.com/life/a36634635/how-to-start-over/

• Mind Fuel Daily. (2018, February 14). *3 good things: An exercise to boost happiness*. Mind Fuel Daily.
https://www.mindfueldaily.com/livewell/3-good-things-an-exercise-to-boost-happiness/

- Mind Tools. (2001, December 27). *Positive thinking, thought awareness, and rational thinking.* Mind Tools. https://www.mindtools.com/pages/article/newTCS_06.htm
- Moore, L. (2021, June 2). *How meditation changes the brain.* Psych Central. https://psychcentral.com/blog/how-meditation-changes-the-brain
- Morin, A. (2015, May 8). *9 ways to get past self-pity.* Psychology Today. https://www.psychologytoday.com/us/blog/what-mentally-strong-people-dont-do/201505/9-ways-get-past-self-pity
- Morin, A. (2020, April 8). *Self-Pity will drain you of the mental strength you need to get through the coronavirus pandemic—here's how to avoid it.* Forbes. https://www.forbes.com/sites/amymorin/2020/04/08/self-pity-is-your-worst-enemy-in-getting-through-this-coronavirus-covid-19-pandemic-heres-how-to-avoid-it/?sh=35f3b27c6120
- Nelson Mandela Quotes. (n.d.). Driven Quote. Retrieved February 20, 2019, from HelloDriven.com: https://home.hellodriven.com/articles/the-50-best-resilience-quotes/
- Northrup, K. (2021, February 11). *How to plan your life when the future is foggy at best.* Harvard Business Review. https://hbr.org/2021/02/how-to-plan-your-life-when-the-future-is-foggy-at-best
- Pangilinan, J. (2022, February 22). *55 hobbies for women to relax and enjoy life.* Happier Human. https://www.happierhuman.com/hobbies-for-women/
- Pietrangelo, A. (2020, July 21). *Understanding self-destructive behavior.* Healthline.

https://www.healthline.com/health/mental-health/self-destructive-behavior

* Raab, D. (2019). *What is emotional wellness?* Psychology Today. https://www.psychologytoday.com/us/blog/the-empowerment-diary/201910/what-is-emotional-wellness

* Ratliff, J. (2017, January 2). *7 things you should do if you want to find your passion.* Medium; Personal Growth. https://medium.com/personal-growth/7-things-you-should-do-if-you-want-to-find-your-passion-af9e96a795cc

* Raypole, C. (2019, September 10). *Big feels and how to talk about them.* Healthline. https://www.healthline.com/health/list-of-emotions

* Raypole, C. (2020a, September 1). *Positive affirmations: Too good to be true?* Healthline. https://www.healthline.com/health/mental-health/do-affirmations-work

* Raypole, C. (2020b, November 13). *How to identify and manage your emotional triggers.* Healthline. https://www.healthline.com/health/mental-health/emotional-triggers

* Resnick, A. (2021, October 26). *What is emotional wellness?* Verywell Mind. https://www.verywellmind.com/emotional-wellness-5206535

* Richo, D. (2006). *The five things we cannot change...and the happiness we find by embracing them.* Shambhala.

* Robbins, T. (2021, February 12). *5 most effective neuro linguistic programming techniques.* Tonyrobbins.com. https://www.tonyrobbins.com/leadership-impact/nlp-techniques/

* Ruane, J. (2012, December 5). *How to let go of resentment and anger.* Lifehack.

https://www.lifehack.org/articles/lifestyle/how-to-le
t-go-of-a-resentment.html
- Ruth, A. (2022, January 16). *8 ways to train your brain to become more positive.* Due.
https://due.com/blog/train-your-brain-to-become-more-positive/
- SAMHSA. (2014). *Understanding the impact of trauma.* Nih.gov; Substance Abuse and Mental Health Services Administration (US).
https://www.ncbi.nlm.nih.gov/books/NBK207191/
- Sandoiu, A. (2018a, February 24). *Self-compassion may protect perfectionists from depression.* Medical News Today.
https://www.medicalnewstoday.com/articles/321024
- Sandoiu, A. (2018b, March 23). *The importance of self-love and how to cultivate it.* Medical News Today.
https://www.medicalnewstoday.com/articles/321309
- Santos-Longhurst, A. (2019, February 21). *Benefits of thinking positively, and how to do it.* Healthline.
https://www.healthline.com/health/how-to-think-positive
- Say, N. (2020, March 24). *6 ways to use affirmations effectively to change your life.* Happier Human.
https://www.happierhuman.com/use-affirmations/
- Schacter, Daniel L., Addis, D., Hassabis, D., Martin, Victoria C., Spreng, R. Nathan, & Szpunar, Karl K. (2012). The future of memory: Remembering, imagining, and the brain. *Neuron, 76*(4), 677–694.
https://doi.org/10.1016/j.neuron.2012.11.001
- Scott, E. (2020, November 18). *What is the law of attraction?* VerywellMind.
https://www.verywellmind.com/understanding-and-u
sing-the-law-of-attraction-3144808
- Scott, E. (2021a, March 19). *The effects of poorly managed anger.* Verywell Mind.

https://www.verywellmind.com/how-anger-problems-can-affect-your-health-3145075

• Scott, E. (2021b, September 17). *Financial stress: How to cope.* Verywell Mind. https://www.verywellmind.com/understanding-and-preventing-financial-stress-3144546

• Scott, E. (2022, February 16). *How negative emotions affect us.* Verywell Mind. https://www.verywellmind.com/embrace-negative-emotions-4158317

• Sehgal, K., & Chopra, D. (2019, April 5). *Do this for 5 minutes every day to rewire your brain for success, according to neuroscience.* CNBC. https://www.cnbc.com/2019/04/03/deepak-chopra-sanjay-gupta-simple-trick-to-training-your-brain-for-success-according-to-neuroscience.html

• Seltzer, L. F. (2017, July 19). *How and why you compromise your integrity.* Psychology Today. https://www.psychologytoday.com/ca/blog/evolution-the-self/201707/how-and-why-you-compromise-your-integrity

• Seneca Quotes. (n.d.). Brainy Quote. Retrieved March 8, 2022, from BrainyQuote.com: https://www.brainyquote.com/quotes/seneca_405078

• Silverton, L. (2020, April 30). *12 types of meditation: A breakdown of the major styles.* Mindbodygreen. https://www.mindbodygreen.com/articles/the-12-major-types-of-meditation-explained-simply

• Stephen Ambrose Quotes. (n.d.). Brainy Quote. Retrieved March 8, 2022, from BrainyQuote.com: https://www.brainyquote.com/quotes/stephen_ambrose_186012

• Stevenson, M. (2017, December 20). *The law of subconscious influence: How to use NLP for*

manifestation. The Law of Attraction.
https://www.thelawofattraction.com/subconscious-inf
luence/

* Stewart, A. R. (2018, September 18). *13 steps to achieving total self-love.* Healthline.
https://www.healthline.com/health/13-self-love-habi
ts-every-woman-needs-to-have

* Stöber, J. (2003). *Self-Pity: Exploring the links to personality, control beliefs, and anger.* Journal of Personality, 71(2), 183–220.
https://doi.org/10.1111/1467-6494.7102004

* Tan, C. (2017, March 17). *Are women harsher towards themselves?* Thrive Global.
https://medium.com/thrive-global/are-women-harsh
er-towards-themselves-a1057eac6063

* Taylor, S. (2013, April 8). *The power of acceptance.* Psychology Today.
https://www.psychologytoday.com/ca/blog/out-the-
darkness/201304/the-power-acceptance

* Team Tony. (2018, April 4). *How to let go of the past: 9 tips for moving on from the past—for good.* Tony Robbins.
https://www.tonyrobbins.com/mind-meaning/let-go
-past/

* Thompson, A. (2007, September 5). *Bad memories stick better than good.* Live Science.
https://www.livescience.com/1827-bad-memories-sti
ck-good.html

* Thorpe, M. (2020, October 27). *12 science-based benefits of meditation.* Healthline.
https://www.healthline.com/nutrition/12-benefits-of
-meditation

* Trickey, G. (2016, August 24). *Self-Criticism could be the biggest barrier to women's success at work.* PCL.

https://www.psychological-consultancy.com/blog/self-criticism-biggest-barrier-womens-success-work/

• Vishnu's Virtues. (2017, June 24). *A simple guide for starting over in life.* Medium. https://vishnusvirtues.medium.com/a-simple-guide-for-starting-over-in-life-d816eed5951e

• Weingus, L. (2019, January 22). *How to let go of anger for your own well-being.* Well+Good. https://www.wellandgood.com/how-to-let-go-anger/

About Author

Lara Spadetto is an Italian author and figurative artist who loves to travel, cook and experiment with her painting. She likes to relax by taking long walks in nature.

After living in Italy, Spain, and UAE, she now lives permanently in the UK with her 3 children and her beloved dog Maia.

She firmly believes that every woman can and should find her own inner strength and be a powerful influence on those around her.

Printed in Great Britain
by Amazon

17659717R00091